# PROBLEMS IN CIVILIZATION

David H. Pinkney

General Editor

PROBLEMS IN CIVILIZATION

# THE RUSSIAN REVOLUTION

Disorder or New Order?

Edited with
an Introduction by

Daniel R. Brower

University of California

FORUM PRESS

Copyright © 1979 by Forum Press, St. Louis, Missouri. All rights reserved. No part of this work may be reproduced or transmitted by any means, electronic or mechanical, including photocopying and recording, or by an information storage or retrieval system without permission in writing from the publisher.

Published simultaneously in Canada.

Printed in the United States of America.

Library of Congress Catalog Card Number: 78-67917

ISBN: 0-88273-406-7

May Day demonstration in Petrograd: on the left, a group of officers supporting the Provisional Government parade under the banner "Long Live the Democratic Republic!"; on the right, workers backing the Petrograd Soviet wave the banner "Long Live Socialism!"

—Photo courtesy of Hoover Institution

# CONTENTS

INTRODUCTION

CHRONOLOGICAL TABLE

CONFLICT OF OPINION

I. POLITICAL LEADERSHIP
    P.V. VOLOBUEV
        *The February Revolution and the Bolshevik Party*      1
    WILLIAM G. ROSENBERG
        *The Instability of Liberal Government*      8
    OSKAR ANWEILER
        *The Ideals of Revolutionary Democracy*      16
    THEODORE H. VON LAUE
        *The Weakness of Governmental Authority*      23
    HARVEY ASHER
        *The Defeat of Military Leadership*      32

II. SOCIAL REVOLUTION AND BOLSHEVIK INSURRECTION
    JOHN L.H. KEEP
        *Revolution in the Factories*      40
    LAZAR VOLIN
        *The Triumph of the Peasantry*      49
    MARC FERRO
        *Citizen-Soldiers in the Revolutionary Struggle*      57
    I.I. MINTS
        *Lenin's Revolutionary Leadership*      67
    ROBERT V. DANIELS
        *The Unpredictable Revolution*      74

CONCLUSION      82

SUGGESTIONS FOR ADDITIONAL READING      85

# INTRODUCTION

THE Russian Revolution has in recent years been the subject of much renewed study. Scholars have explored topics previously ignored, while others have questioned assumptions earlier accepted as fact. From their research have come a large number of important books and articles which expand and deepen our understanding of the revolution. They have also enhanced our appreciation for the complexity of the forces at work in Russia in 1917. Disagreement has not disappeared on the causes and significance of key events. The views of Soviet historians differ markedly from those of most Western scholars, the latter of whom argue among themselves on basic questions of interpretation. This book of readings includes excerpts from some of these recent works. It focuses on the period from February to October, 1917, examining in each selection issues and events important in interpreting the nature and outcome of the revolution.

The question on which this book focuses its attention derives from the very meaning given the word "revolution," usually defined as the violent overthrow of one political system and its replacement by another. Disorder has always been a part of major revolutions, as political groups struggle for power and social classes fight for wealth and influence. In Russia the conflict reached massive proportions, a fact which has led some historians to argue (as did some of the political leaders in 1917) that the revolution was anarchic. In this view the Bolshevik regime represented a separate stage of the revolution, for it imposed by force its own institutions and leadership on a country in complete disintegration. Our definition of revolution suggests also the possibility that the new order emerges in the midst of the collapse of the old. The apparent disorder could thus hide creative social and political forces at work laying the foundations for a new state. Historians have pointed out that in 1917 the popular assemblies called "soviets" appeared along with other mass revolutionary organizations immediately or soon after the fall of the autocracy, and ultimately provided the framework for the new Bolshevik order. Soviet writers argue that the working classes, whose interests the soviets defended, were the real force of the revolution and the basis for the Bolshevik triumph. The question the reader should keep in mind is thus whether the revolution produced the breakdown of all political institutions or whether the structure of a new revolutionary regime was formed in the midst of chaos — in other words, whether the revolution was essentially a destructive or constructive event. An answer to that question can provide the key to interpreting the entire revolution.

This problem can be divided into two distinct but closely connected issues, one relating to political leadership in the course of the revolution, the other to the social upheaval. In part, the chances for a peaceful transfer of power depended upon the ability of groups and individuals aspiring to political command. The tsar had lost all claim to legitimate authority; would any heir — liberals, democratic socialists, radicals, or the military — be able to win sufficient support behind their program for the reconstruction of the country to establish durable control of the state? In part, too, the direction which the revolution took depended upon the behavior of the lower classes. This issue was particularly important since so many Russian men had in the course of the war been called to arms, at the front or in the garrison towns. Their political attitudes, if translated into armed demonstrations, had an immediate impact on public life. In addition, peasants and workers had deep and abiding grievances against the old order which they sought to remedy when the tsar's fall brought freedom to the country. Would they heed the call of political parties to follow an orderly process of reforming society and the economy, or would they take

# INTRODUCTION

matters into their own hands, defying all political controls and thereby transforming freedom into anarchy? Related to this question is the problem of the relationship between the mass revolution and the October (Bolshevik) Revolution. Was the rise of Lenin's party the result of the Bolsheviks' ability as vanguard of the proletariat to give voice and leadership to the country's working classes, or was it the product of the organizational and agitational ability of a tiny band of professional revolutionaries ready to exploit a political vacuum of power? The issues of leadership and mass agitation provide the themes for the two sections into which the readings are divided. Though each author discusses a different topic, his interpretation throws important light on one or the other of these issues; when taken altogether, their views offer the reader a broad sampling of recent scholarly opinions on the revolution.

Why does disagreement remain so great among scholars studying the Russian Revolution? The reason lies partially in the very nature of the event, so profound and complex that it defies simple explanation. It began as a revolt against Tsar Nicholas II, but quickly assumed the dimensions of a social revolution involving millions of Russians and non-Russians in the Empire. Historians can on very legitimate grounds debate the relative importance of mass movements and political leadership in seeking to explain the reasons for the path taken by the revolution. However, another important reason for differing interpretations is found in the ideological perception which historians bring to their study of the revolution. Marxism-Leninism provides a precise class interpretation to which all Soviet historians adhere. Debate is limited to questions of fact, though even here the margin of discussion is narrow. One of the Soviet historians whose views are presented here, P.V. Volobuev, was seriously criticized by his colleagues for having raised a factual issue which in Western eyes appears so obvious as not to merit debate. Western historians are free to choose their views, approaching their subjects from a wide variety of intellectual and ideological perspectives. Thus, Marc Ferro can credit the attitudes and behavior of the Russian soldiers as having played an important part in the development of the revolution, which he views in his writings as largely the product of mass movements. Robert Daniels, on the other hand, can argue that the Bolshevik Revolution was a political gamble, since he excludes the possibility of any historical "laws" and discounts the ability of a "Great Man," in this case Lenin, to control a tumultuous revolutionary conflict.

To understand properly the issues in the readings, it is worthwhile to review briefly the events which led up to and highlighted the revolution. Before 1917 Russia had already experienced one massive revolution. In 1905 a combination of worker and peasant violence, plus a strong liberal movement, had challenged the autocracy, which until then had assured the tsar absolute power over his enormous empire. This absolute monarchy, the last one remaining among the major European states, could not withstand the pressure of the opposition, which was particularly effective in October, when the Russian workers declared a general strike and supported the liberal demands for representative government and civil and political liberties. At the same time they formed their own urban representative institutions, the soviets, made up of delegates from the factories in many of the towns and cities paralyzed by the strike. Out of this revolution emerged a modified autocracy in which Tsar Nicholas granted some of his male subjects the right to vote for representatives to a legislative assembly, the Duma. The powers of this assembly were severely restricted; control over policies and appointments remained in the hands of the tsar. Still, fundamental laws allowed legal parties to play an active role in political life for a few years. The leading liberal party in the Duma was the Constitutional Democratic (shortened usually to Cadet) party, whose leader was Paul Miliukov.

Disputing the liberals' leadership were three socialist parties. One of these, the Socialist Revolutionary (SR) party, was an

# INTRODUCTION

authentic, very disorganized product of the Russian populist revolutionary movement; it claimed to defend the interests of the working masses by seeking a real democratic republic and sweeping social reforms, the most important of which was land reform for the peasantry. For having taken an active and often violent part in the revolution of 1905, most of its leaders spent the following years in exile or in prison. The Marxist Social Democratic (SD) party was by this time irrevocably split between two factions. One, the Mensheviks, sought under the leadership of men like Julius Martov to organize and defend the working class during the period of bourgeois democracy which they felt had to come (following Marx's historical schema) before the country was ready for socialism. The other was the Bolshevik party under Vladimir Lenin, who had become convinced as a result of the 1905 revolution that the tempo of Russian history could be accelerated through a revolutionary-democratic regime in which his small but disciplined party could play the part of vanguard of the proletariat.

The outbreak of World War I in 1914 soon brought to a head the political and social conflicts which divided the country. The army proved to be no match for the German forces, which by 1916 occupied a large part of the western region of the Empire. Many Russian patriots (including the Cadets) thought that the tsar, now dominated by his wife Alexandra and by Rasputin, was incapable of leading the country in its hour of crisis. In addition, the economy was unable to provide for the tremendous demands of the Russian war machine and still supply the basic needs of the Russian urban population, enormously increased by the influx of war refugees from the west. The capital of the Empire, then called Petrograd, was particularly vulnerable to these pressures. There the Cadet party demanded in the Duma a new, vigorous government responsive to the wishes of the nation; there the industrial work force was increasingly rebellious for both political and economic reasons; there the long, cold, northern winter accentuated the dependence upon the railroads for food and coal to keep the city's two million inhabitants alive.

The breaking point was reached in the winter of 1916-17. It is probable that even without the war and German military victories, fundamental political changes would have occurred; the real question was whether these would come by evolutionary or revolutionary means. The crisis of February 1917 resolved that issue, for it took only one week for bread riots and strikes in Petrograd to turn into political demonstrations, mutiny of regiments of the Petrograd garrison, and the downfall of the Russian autocracy. This unexpectedly swift revolution forced the presumptive political heirs to the tsar to step forward or lose their chance to guide the country at a crucial period. The Cadet party was instrumental in forming a provisional government, appointed largely from Duma deputies, whose task it was to rule the country temporarily until a new constitutional order would be created by a democratically elected constituent assembly. The war had, of course, to go on until resolved by multilateral peace negotiations; all patriots agreed on that.

Alongside the Provisional Government appeared the Petrograd Soviet, made up this time of representatives of the garrison as well as of the factory workers of the city. Its Executive Committee was composed of Menshevik and SR leaders, whose decision it was to support the Provisional Government. These same men took leadership of the nationwide soviet movement which quickly coalesced, and they assumed the dominant role in the Central Executive Committee chosen by the First All-Russian Congress of Soviets in June. They were to hold these positions until replaced by Bolsheviks, first in the Petrograd Soviet Executive Committee in September, then in the Central Executive Committee at the Second Congress of Soviets at the very moment of the October Revolution. The coexistence of these two sources of political authority, the one appointed by the Duma (now virtually defunct), the other supported by the lower urban classes, created a unique political situation described at the time as "dual power."

# INTRODUCTION

The authority of the Provisional Government was challenged seriously several times in the months that followed the February Revolution. The first came in April, and was provoked by a dispute over war aims in which the Foreign Minister, the Cadet Paul Miliukov, suggested that the new regime should pursue the tsarist policy of peace with territorial annexations, while political opponents in the soviet and demonstrators in the streets of Petrograd protested vigorously in favor of a peace with no annexations. Miliukov had to resign his ministry, and to save the authority of the government the Petrograd Soviet's Executive Committee authorized some of its members to participate in a coalition cabinet. The new Provisional Government, uniting socialists and liberals, maintained the same internal policies as before, however.

Rising unrest among the proletariat in Petrograd and in part of the garrison and naval forces stationed at the nearby fortress of Kronstadt led to the next crisis in July. The Bolshevik party backed the demonstrators' demands for soviet power, although its central leadership did so unwillingly. Military units supporting the moderate, democratic socialist leadership of the Petrograd Soviet were responsible for the defeat of the demonstrations, following which Bolshevik leaders were ordered arrested (Lenin escaped to Finland). Out of this crisis came a new Prime Minister, Alexander Kerensky. However, in late August the new commander-in-chief, General Kornilov, attempted to take over the government by force to restore order in the country. Kerensky mobilized popular forces, including those of the newly respectable Bolshevik party, to defeat Kornilov. Soon afterwards he began to lose the support of the soviets, which in early September shifted their support to the Bolshevik revolutionary program.

The Bolshevik party had been in existence as a separate Marxist faction for slightly over a decade. It had evolved a distinct organization, headed by a Central Committee made up of Lenin's most trusted supporters, including Kamenev, Zinoviev, and Joseph Stalin. Added to the committee in mid-1917 was the young Marxist maverick, Leon Trotsky, who previously had fought Lenin bitterly but now joined forces for the sake of the proletarian revolution. Ever since he had returned in April from exile in Switzerland, Lenin had proclaimed the readiness of his party to assume leadership of a revolutionary democratic regime. The "July Days" appeared to have dealt a fatal setback to his plans, but the Kornilov *putsch* gave his party renewed strength as defender of the revolution, just as it served to augment in severity and scope the social revolution among factory workers and the peasantry. The essential issue confronting the party in the fall of 1917 was whether to seize power independently or to work in conjunction with other socialist groups within the soviets. Zinoviev and Kamenev headed the group favoring the latter policy, while from early September Lenin urged the former policy. In early October he finally won over a majority in the Central Committee in favor of armed insurrection. Shortly thereafter, the Bolshevik leaders of the Petrograd Soviet backed the creation of the Military Revolutionary Committee of the Soviet, ostensibly to fight the counterrevolution, in reality to gather together Bolshevik forces. On October 22 the Military Revolutionary Committee placed the Petrograd garrison completely under its command. The revolutionary process had begun, which would lead to the overthrow of the Provisional Government on October 25 and the creation of a Bolshevik government in the name of soviet power.

The readings that follow examine important issues and trends appearing in the course of the Revolution. The first five selections concentrate on the problems of political leadership in the spring and summer. The Soviet historian P.V. Volobuev asserts that the February Revolution was the necessary outcome of the historical development of his country in the early twentieth century. Using the rigorous conceptual approach of Marxism-Leninism, he argues that in the conditions of expanding capitalism, the Russian bourgeoisie had basic class interests contradictory to those of the feudal,

# INTRODUCTION

landlord class and of the tsarist regime. Only a bourgeois revolution could eliminate these contradictions. There were of course "peculiarities" which made the February Revolution unique, chief among which was the leading role of the working masses. February was thus a bourgeois-democratic revolution. The Menshevik and SR leaders of the Petrograd Soviet, allies of the bourgeoisie, were incapable of carrying out the proletarian revolution which these special conditions made possible. Only the Bolsheviks, vanguard of the proletariat, could lead the country on to a new, higher stage of historical development.

Disagreeing with Volobuev, William Rosenberg presents the February Revolution as primarily a political conflict. Though he too argues that the liberals were unwilling revolutionaries, he sees the reason for this in the war against the Central Powers. The Cadet Leadership sought above all a national political leadership to maintain unity and to strengthen the war effort. The pressure of the masses in the soviets forced them to abandon any hope of preserving the monarchy and the Duma. Instead, they were obliged to form a Provisional Government, whose most important immediate task was to pursue the war. This concern above all led them to defer any substantial reforms, though for the sake of the authority of the government they had to collaborate with the socialist leaders of the soviets. From the very start, thus, their power rested on fragile foundations.

Why in fact did the forces of revolutionary democracy, the Menshevik and SR leaders of the Petrograd Soviet, fail to seize power in the first months of the revolution? Oskar Anweiler does not find them, as does Volobuev, tools of the liberals, nor does he believe them political incompetents. He asserts that they were radical intellectuals suddenly thrust into a politically chaotic situation with no experience in public affairs and little actual control over the masses. They were not overly preoccupied with the ideological issue of a "bourgeois" stage of the revolution, much more with practical considerations of dealing with the war in a very divided country. They hoped to control and guide the Provisional Government toward a democratic peace and the gradual expansion of revolutionary policies, seeking to preserve order by collaborating with the liberals.

These moderate political aims failed, in the opinion of Theodore Von Laue, to take into account the weakness of the new regime. He looks at Russia in 1917 as a country experiencing the pressures and conflicts of Westernization, in which the forces tending toward disorder were far greater than the central political authority generated by democratic institutions. The new government confronted monumental problems in trying to provide food for the population and to maintain economic production. It failed in both tasks. Von Laue argues that its failure was due largely to the conflicting social forces in the country, which would not voluntarily submit to central control. In his view, unity and strength could be achieved only by a new dictatorship.

Once in the course of the revolution the military sought to introduce their own type of order. Harvey Asher examines the complex chain of events leading up to the revolt of General Kornilov, paying particular attention to the role of Alexander Kerensky. He finds the origin of the revolt to be Kornilov's efforts toward reinstituting order in the crumbling Russian army, a policy which attracted wide support from those eager to restore order in the political life of the country. Asher asserts that Kerensky himself sought military support in his effort to control the political extremists, but turned against Kornilov when he came to believe the general was going to remove him from power. Issues faded from view in a personal struggle for power. This dispute between the military and civilian leaders of the country doomed the military coup to failure and, Asher implies, benefited only the Bolsheviks.

The remaining five readings analyze the nature and extent of the social revolution in 1917 and the rise of the Bolshevik party to power in October. John Keep suggests that the working class movement was in the first months independent of political groups claiming to speak for the proletariat. The workers, in his opinion, were at heart hostile to capitalism, but at the beginning of the Revolution sought primarily the improvement of their living and working conditions. Strikes and the formation of factory committees had these goals originally. Their effect was to increase disorder and violence in the country, however, as economic conditions worsened and employers curtailed production and even closed their factories. Keep argues that the worker militia was also non-party at its origin, an expression of the workers' desire to fight the counterrevolution. After the Kornilov revolt, the Bolsheviks could exploit the workers' political militancy to win their support. The working class movement was in this perspective ultimately destructive, since it disregarded moderate leadership and naively backed the party that "promised untold blessings once 'soviet power' had been achieved."

Lazar Volin views the revolt in the countryside, on the other hand, as an avoidable development had the Provisional Government acted quickly on agrarian reform. The peasantry had taken no direct part in the February Revolution and did not engage in violent acts in the first months. Volin feels, however, that the old peasant desire to divide all the arable land among themselves was as powerful as ever. By not recognizing this fact and acting on it the government lost whatever authority it had in the countryside and played into the hands of the Bolshevik party. Upon assuming power, Lenin granted the peasants the right to seize and divide up all large farms, thus sanctioning the illegal and frequently violent rural revolution already under way. The responsibility for this outcome, in Volin's opinion, lies in the inaction of the democratic leadership of the revolution.

The most potent mass force in 1917 was the Russian soldiers, who in the opinion of Marc Ferro became "citizen-soldiers" that year. Their arms and military training gave them the power to affect decisively the political struggle, either by intervening directly through armed demonstrations or by abstaining from action. Ferro asserts that the mass of front-line soldiers remained patriotic, ready to defend their country against the German and Austrian invaders, but that they gave their loyalty to the Petrograd Soviet, not to the Provisional Government. They were revolutionary in that they sought to moderate the ruthless discipline of the tsarist army, and became more so as they encountered the opposition of the Russian officer corps. Above all, they wished for peace. The failure of the moderate Soviet leadership to bring an end to the hostilities and the rising fear of counterrevolution, apparent in the reaction to the June offensive and the Kornilov revolt, led them to turn in greater and greater numbers to the Bolshevik party. Ferro suggests that these citizen-soldiers represented a decisive revolutionary force whose swing to the left provided solid foundations for the Bolshevik revolutionary movement.

In the view of I.I. Mints, the growing support for the Bolshevik party among the masses by the late summer of 1917 proved the correctness of Lenin's perception of the revolutionary process and of the Bolshevik leader's program for immediate armed insurrection. He quotes extensively from Lenin's letters sent in September to the party leadership, to show the accuracy and detail of the program for insurrection. Mints recognizes that certain party leaders did not share Lenin's confidence in the success of a Bolshevik seizure of power, but he treats them as a misguided minority of "legalists" who did not understand that the proletarian revolution demanded forceful action at that particular moment. The decision of the Central Committee on October 10 to support the policy of armed insurrection represents for Mints conclusive evidence of the unity of the party under Lenin's brilliant leadership.

Robert Daniels presents a very different picture of the party during the days in late October when the conflict with the Provisional Government had reached a crisis. The party, in his opinion, remained seriously divided over the question of insurrection. Its leaders in Petrograd were primarily concerned to defend it from Kerensky's attack

# INTRODUCTION

while awaiting for the Second Congress of Soviets, where they counted on forming a coalition government. The Bolshevik members of the Soviet's Military Revolutionary Committee, including Leon Trotsky, were mobilizing their military supporters for action, but had no plan of attack on the government until Lenin emerged from hiding on the night of October 24-25 to take direct command of his party. Daniels emphasizes particularly the unexpected feebleness of the Provisional Government's troops, who proved unable to resist even the small forces launched against them by the Bolshevik party. In his view their weakness was as much responsible for the success of the October Revolution as Lenin's dynamic leadership. The Bolshevik seizure of power appears in this light as a revolution by default.

In examining the selections that follow, the reader should keep in mind that the Russian Revolution was a series of revolutions and revolts of extraordinary violence and complexity. The hopes and ambitions of millions of Russians, repressed for so long, suddenly seemed near to fulfillment. The country lived an incredible adventure in those few months, at the end of which some Russians felt that they had achieved the real revolution, while others believed that a terrible tragedy had befallen their country. The debate continues — as do the effects of this revolution — one of the most significant in modern history. One cannot comprehend the course of events of the twentieth century without studying the Russian Revolution. These readings provide merely an introduction to the major issues of this revolution.

## A Note on Dates

Most writings on the Russian Revolution employ the dates of the "Old Style" Julian calendar then in use in Russia, which was thirteen days behind the "New Style" Gregorian calendar in the West. Thus, the February Revolution took place according to the Western calendar in March, the October Revolution in November. Unless otherwise indicated, all dates used here will be those of the Old Style calendar.

# CHRONOLOGICAL TABLE

| Old Style | New Style | |
|---|---|---|
| January 31 | February 12 | Beginning of a new strike wave in Petrograd |
| February 22–March 2 | March 7–15 | February Revolution |
| February 26 | March 11 | First mutinies in Petrograd garrison |
| February 27 | March 12 | Formation of Temporary Duma Committee and of Petrograd Soviet |
| March 1 | March 14 | Petrograd Soviet issues Order Number I to garrison |
| March 2 | March 15 | Abdication of Nicholas II; formation of Provisional Government |
| March 25 | April 7 | Government decree on grain monopoly |
| April 3 | April 16 | Lenin arrives in Petrograd |
| April 20–21 | May 3–4 | "April Days": Demonstrations in Petrograd and Moscow against Miliukov's declaration of annexationist war aims |
| May 5 | May 18 | Formation of First Coalition Government with participation of socialists from Petrograd Soviet |
| May 30–June 3 | June 12–16 | First conference of Petrograd factory committees supports Bolshevik policies |
| June 3–24 | June 16–July 7 | First All-Russian Congress of Workers' and Soldiers' Soviets |
| June 18–28 | July 1–11 | Military offensive on Austrian front |
| July 3–5 | July 16–18 | "July Days": Mass demonstrations in Petrograd for "all power to soviets"; Bolshevik leaders arrested, Lenin in hiding in Finland |
| July 12 | July 25 | Provisional Government re-establishes death penalty in army |
| July 18 | July 31 | General Kornilov appointed commander-in-chief |
| July 24 | August 6 | Formation of Second Coalition, Kerensky Prime Minister |
| August 12–15 | August 25–28 | Moscow State Conference |
| August 26–30 | September 8–12 | Kornilov revolt |
| August 31 | September 13 | Bolsheviks gain majority in Petrograd Soviet |
| September 5 | September 18 | Bolsheviks gain majority in Moscow Soviet |

CHRONOLOGICAL TABLE

| | | |
|---|---|---|
| September 14-22 | September 27–October 5 | Democratic Conference |
| September 23 | October 6 | Trotsky elected chairman of Petrograd Soviet |
| September 25 | October 8 | Formation of Third Coalition |
| October 7 | October 20 | First meeting of Council of the Republic, boycotted by Bolsheviks |
| October 10 | October 23 | Bolshevik Central Committee approves Lenin's resolution on armed insurrection |
| October 12 | October 25 | Petrograd Soviet approves formation of Military Revolutionary Committee |
| October 24-25 | November 6-7 | October Revolution: Military Revolutionary Committee overthrows Provisional Government |
| October 26 | November 8 | Second Congress of Soviets approves all-Bolshevik Council of People's Commissars and "soviet power" |

# CONFLICT OF OPINION

I. POLITICAL LEADERSHIP

"No one had organized and no one had foreseen . . . the spontaneous revolutionary outbreak which occurred on February 23 and marked the beginning of the revolution. . . . Under these conditions the Petrograd organization [of the Bolshevik party] could not bring under its leadership the growing revolutionary avalanche. . . . The revolutionary proletariat was overwhelmed both intellectually and numerically by the petty bourgeoisie, whose views were expressed by the Mensheviks and SRs. . . . In these conditions, the better organized liberal bourgeoisie had no difficulty seizing power from the revolutionary masses."

— P.V. VOLOBUEV

"Reflecting the Petrograd Kadet ethos, the new provisional regime was decidedly 'nonpartisan' in all of its initial pronouncements, officially committing itself to national rather than sectarian interests. But it was hardly representative. Instead it reflected the emphasis on elite rather than mass politics . . . ; it was concerned with political, not social democracy; and it reflected the intense desire to win the war and advance Russia's 'national interests' which had largely impelled all of the Kadets' own policies in the preceding two and one-half years."

— WILLIAM G. ROSENBERG

"Trotsky spoke of 'the paradox of the February Revolution,' referring to the voluntary renunciation by the Petrograd Soviet of the seizure of power by the revolutionary democracy, possible at the time of the fall of the monarch. On closer examination, however, this thesis proves fictitious. . . . That handful of socialist intellectuals, whose very names were hardly familiar to the public, grew frightened of the burden of power, feeling that exercise of government demands more than a few revolutionary ideas and skillful tactics."

— OSKAR ANWEILER

"Thus the peoples of Russia, with unprecedented suddenness, were propelled into the age of mass politics and thrust up, unprepared, against the problem of reconstituting their government by voluntary agreement. . . . The sudden grant of full freedom encouraged among all layers of the population a penchant for unilateral and precipitous action not cleared with the Provisional Government. . . . Wherever one looked in Russia in these months, authority and anarchy were closely intertwined, and any effort to create or assert authority often aggravated the anarchy."

— THEODORE H. VON LAUE

"Was there a Kornilov revolt? The answer is yes. . . . Kornilov was prepared to march against the Bolsheviks without the support of the Provisional Government. . . . Since his sympathies lay with the moderate

CONFLICT OF OPINION

left, Kerensky hesitated to enact stern measures which might unduly excite public opinion, even though he recognized the necessity of halting the disintegration of the army. Thus Kerensky vacillated, wanting to support Kornilov's program, yet fearing it might lead to a dictatorship of the Right.... The struggle which ensued was waged between men and not ideas."

— HARVEY ASHER

II. SOCIAL REVOLUTION AND BOLSHEVIK INSURRECTION

"The collapse of tsarism was the signal for militant action on a hitherto unparalleled scale by an ever-growing segment of Russia's labor force. The sudden disappearance of the old regime raised intoxicating hopes of a new golden age.... The scope of their demands quickly escalated until their cumulative force amounted to a call for a new system of industrial relations.... These demands could not be wholly satisfied by any of the parties or groups active in Russian political life during 1917; even the Bolshevik programme did not do justice to the almost apocalyptic hopes engendered among a broad segment of their clientele."

— JOHN L.H. KEEP

"There could be no question that the young Russian democracy was being confronted with a sweeping peasant revolt that gained in violence with the passage of time and was no less formidable because of its unorganized character.... This was a ferocious, primitive, and contagious peasant war.... But this does not mean that the peasants were influenced by such slogans as the demand for abolition of private property and socialization of land. To the peasant rank and file, socialization had at best a purely pragmatic value as a convenient formula for land seizure."

— LAZAR VOLIN

"Bolsheviks without realizing it, the discontented soldiers began to take an interest in the party's propaganda. It was the only party that approved the soldiers' actions, and the course of events had not ceased to prove their predictions right. Gradually the troops adopted their slogans, and from mid-July onward Bolshevization of the army proceeded apace, especially after the failure of the Kornilov putsch."

— MARC FERRO

"Bourgeois falsifiers carefully avoid the basic fact that almost 85 percent of the members of the Central Committee supported Lenin's proposal for an immediate insurrection. One can find in history few examples of similar unanimity on the eve of such a major, decisive turning point as the shift of the party to a direct attack on the old order and to the creation of a new society.... This unanimity can be explained by the entire previous history of the party, by the unity of its theoretical and organizational views, inspired and organized by the work of Lenin."

— I.I. MINTS

CONFLICT OF OPINION

"The facts of the record show that in the crucial days before October 24th Lenin was not making his leadership effective.... Kerensky's ill-conceived countermove was the decisive accident. Galvanizing all the fears that the revolutionaries had acquired in July and August about a rightest *putsch*, it brought out their utmost ... effort to defend themselves and hold the ground for the coming Congress of Soviets. With undreamed-of ease, and no intention before the fact, they had the city in the palms of their hands, ready to close their grip when their leader reappeared from the underground...."

— ROBERT DANIELS

# I. POLITICAL LEADERSHIP

## P. V. Volobuev

## THE FEBRUARY REVOLUTION AND THE BOLSHEVIK PARTY

P. V. Volobuev belonged in recent years to the leading group of Soviet historians studying the Revolution of 1917. Though a committed Marxist-Leninist, he still tried to introduce new elements into the Soviet picture of the February Revolution, particularly by suggesting that the Bolsheviks did not control the revolutionary workers. For these slightly heretical views he was dismissed in 1974 from his position as director of the Institute of the History of the USSR in the Academy of Sciences.

IN GENERAL historical terms the February Revolution belongs in the category of bourgeois revolutions. As is widely recognized, the character of a revolution is defined by the objective content of those problems which it is called upon to resolve. The fundamental social content of the February Revolution, its main problem and goal, was the completion of the historically inevitable bourgeois transformation of Russia.

However, the classification of the February Revolution as a bourgeois revolution still does not fully answer the question of its character, even less of its historical peculiarities. At least two other factors have to be taken into account to understand completely the concrete social content of a revolution. The first is the historical period in which the revolution took place; the second is the degree of participation in it by the lower classes. Since the February Revolution occurred in the twentieth century, in the period of imperialism, Marxist historiography defines it, in contrast to the earlier bourgeois revolutions of the seventeenth to nineteenth centuries, as a belated bourgeois revolution. Because the lower classes — proletariat and peasantry — not only took an active part but also provided its principal force, giving it a popular, democratic character, it is universally considered among our historians as a bourgeois-democratic revolution. . . .

Let us now examine, again from a methodological point of view, the question of the peculiarities of the February Revolution. It is necessary to take into account first, the uniqueness of the historical period, and second, the actual historical conditions of the country. Only in this manner, incidentally, is it possible to solve the problem of the dominant forces of the revolution. . . . The Mensheviks[1] mistook the dominant forces of the Russian Revolution precisely because they deviated from the principle of Marxist concreteness in analyzing the actual historical situation. They argued that since this revolution was bourgeois, its leadership

---

1. Marxist opponents of Lenin and of his tactics in 1917 of immediate seizure of power from the Provisional Government – Ed.

From P.V. Volobuev, "Kharakter i osobennosti Fevral'skoi revoliutsii [The character and peculiarities of the February Revolution]," in I.I. Mints (ed.), *Sverzhenie samoderzhaviia* [The overthrow of the autocracy] (Moscow, 1970), pp. 24-38. Translated by the editor. The author's footnotes in this and subsequent selections have been omitted.

and dominant force should be the bourgeoisie. On the other hand, the Bolsheviks understood the role of the proletariat as the leader of the bourgeois-democratic revolution because of their analysis of Russian conditions in the early twentieth century — the distribution and dynamics of class forces in the country.

Having defined the criteria for explaining the peculiarities of the February Revolution, we have established a sound basis on which to compare it with the early bourgeois revolutions and with the first Russian revolution. The revolution of 1905-1907 and the February Revolution share the characteristic that both took place in the same historical period — the period of imperialism. Capitalist Russia entered the twentieth century with the heavy burden of such remnants of its medieval past as landlord agriculture, tsarist absolutism, and nationalist oppression. The first Russian revolution, which should have freed the country from these historical obstructions, failed in its tasks. Therefore, the February Revolution confronted the same objective tasks: to liquidate the remnants of feudalism and to lead the country on the road to broad, free social-economic progress. However, by comparison with the revolution of 1905-1907, the February Revolution occurred in conditions of a higher level of capitalist development and immeasurably more mature class and political relations in the cities and the countryside.... The establishment of monopolistic capitalism in Russia at the beginning of the twentieth century and particularly its expansion in the period of prewar industrial growth showed even more clearly the incompatibility of bourgeois development of the country with a semi-feudal order. Lenin's picture [of Russia] with "the most backward agriculture, the most barbaric countryside, and the most advanced industry and finance capitalism" indicates the profound need and inevitability of the bourgeois-democratic transformation.

In the period between the two revolutions the conflicts in the political life of the country did not lessen, but, on the contrary, worsened. By concluding a political and economic alliance with the upper bourgeoisie, the tsarist regime widened the social base of its rule but could not increase in strength after the blows of the first Russian revolution. The attempt of tsardom to transform itself into a bourgeois monarchy, though partially implemented (Stolypin's agrarian policies[2]), was a failure. The tsarist monarchy on the eve of the First World War was not actually evolving toward a bourgeois order; rather, it was falling apart and decaying at the roots because of its own sluggishness and backwardness and because of the revolutionary conditions in the country. By attempting to introduce bourgeois reforms and proving itself incapable of doing so, the tsarist regime only increased the number of unresolved problems.

During the revolution of 1905-1907 and also during the prewar revolutionary wave, the Russian bourgeoisie became conscious of the strength of the revolutionary proletariat and its capacity to lead a bourgeois-democratic revolution, and therefore became even more counterrevolutionary. However, it had difficulty getting along with "barbaric landlords" in spite of its adaptability to the established order, the similarity of its interests with those of the landlords, and its servility toward the tsar. "The interests of capitalism," [Lenin wrote], "though predatory and parasitic, are not compatible with the undivided rule of feudal landlords." At the same time, the bourgeoisie was deathly afraid of a new revolution and was its determined opponent. Its irritation and displeasure at the incapacity of the regime to introduce minimal bourgeois reforms arose in large measure from their fear of revolution. As the Octobrist leader A. I. Guchkov[3] recalled, even before the war he had lost faith in the possibility of peaceful evolution for Russia.

2. Policies instituted in 1907 by the tsarist government to strengthen the class of independent, well-to-do farmers — Ed.

3. A leading liberal in the Russian pre-revolutionary parliament, the Duma, and member of the first Provisional Government — Ed.

As far as the revolutionary-democratic forces — the proletariat and the peasantry — are concerned, one should note that they acquired in the revolution of 1905-1907 a great amount of revolutionary experience, particularly experience in massive revolutionary action. The Bolshevik party worked hard in the period between the two revolutions to spread among the masses the lessons of the revolution, and kept up the revolutionary awareness of the proletariat. It tirelessly prepared them for the role of leader of the new revolution. It is not surprising, therefore, that despite a certain decline in the level of political awareness of the proletarian masses in the war years, the proletariat stood in this respect on the eve of the February Revolution immeasurably higher than just before 1905.... The slogans presented by the masses in the first days of the February Revolution, starting with the elementary demand "Bread!" and ending with "Down with tsarist autocracy!," were revolutionary slogans.

The outbreak of revolution in Russia was delayed by the beginning of World War I. The war speeded up developments so much, however, that the people demanded an accounting not only of the tsarist regime, but in a short while of Russian capitalism as well. The principal influence which the war had on social-political developments was to hasten the beginning of the triumphant bourgeois-democratic revolution and its evolution into a socialist revolution. Simultaneously, it created such conditions that, in Lenin's words, "the carriage of the Romanov monarchy, overflowing with blood and filth, could completely collapse at any moment."

This occurred mainly because the unresolved tasks of the bourgeois-democratic revolution were augmented by the problems created as a result of the First World War. The first order of the day became the necessity of organizing a war economy and of mobilizing in an orderly manner (under capitalist conditions) all the material, human, and spiritual forces of the nation for the conduct of a great war.... This task was obviously beyond the capacity of the clumsy bureaucratic apparatus of tsarism — remnant of an earlier historical epoch. Though Russian capitalism did in its turn make a significant step forward, approaching a state-monopolistic form, its productive-technical base was too weak to support the demands of a long, intensive war. As a result the tsarist army was doomed to defeat, and the country fated to economic collapse. The burden of war and the internal crisis fell very unevenly on the Russian population, affecting primarily the workers and peasants. Related to this, there occurred a worsening of the class contradictions and class struggle, especially between the working class and the capitalists.

Consequently, the conflict between the demands of the social-economic development of bourgeois Russia, the needs and hopes of her people, and the unbelievably outmoded class-political system became extremely acute during the war years. This fundamental contradiction was the principal motor force of the second bourgeois-democratic revolution in Russia.

... What were the basic political forces, or political camps, whose struggle determined the outcome of the February Revolution? They were: first, the feudal landlords headed by the tsarist monarchy; second, the liberal bourgeoisie and allied landlords; and third, revolutionary democracy — the proletariat and petty bourgeoisie, which was represented mainly by the peasantry. These three were active for the entire period of the bourgeois-democratic revolution in Russia.

As a result of the revolution of 1905-1907 and the subsequent counterrevolution, there occurred a sharp delimitation and self-awareness of all the classes and groups both within these camps and among them. In addition, the war modified considerably the distribution of class and political forces. Thus, the leadership of the Menshevik and SR[4] parties linked themselves more closely to the bourgeoisie by adopting the policies of national defense and social

---

4. Socialist Revolutionary party whose program proposed a special Russian type of socialism for the benefit of peasants as well as workers — Ed.

chauvinism. Joining them were segments of the landlord class, distressed at the political course of the governing elite.

On the eve of the revolution, the positions, aims, and policy of each of the three camps were fully developed. The tsarist regime, head of the class of feudal landlords and bureaucracy, entered a period of crisis and outright decomposition. As a result of military defeats it lost all moral-political credit in the country and deprived itself of the support of part of its own class. A court party of adventurers and reactionaries guided its internal and external policies, which took on an increasingly backward character, and attempted at any price to preserve their exclusive hold over the state. Consequently, tsarism refused any deal with the liberal bourgeoisie, feeling that it could not strengthen its unstable position while it lacked a wide social base in the country. "We see," wrote Lenin on the tactics of tsarism, "the clear position of the monarchy and noble landlords: 'Don't give up' Russia to the liberal bourgeoisie; better [to make] a deal with the German monarchy."

The position and policies of the liberal bourgeoisie on the eve of the February Revolution resembled strongly those of 1905. Lenin characterized in the following manner the essence of its position in 1917: "Because it feared the people more than the reactionaries, it moved toward political control by means of compromise with the monarchy." It is, however, even more significant to note that on the eve of the February Revolution the conflict between the bourgeoisie and tsarism, while not deep and insurmountable, generated *"only* by the immediate situation and the turn of events in the imperialist war," was nonetheless more acute than in 1905. As a result the bourgeoisie had by the end of 1916 become a fierce opponent of tsarism. Its reasons for this were more than sufficient. It was dissatisfied at the military defeats of tsarism, and at the inability to achieve its imperialist program. Bourgeois circles were nervous ... of a separate peace with ... nificantly strengthened both ... economically during the war years, the bourgeoisie had no objection to taking a greater share of political power. It was also incited to oppositionist struggle with the tsarist state by the desire to take over the state-monopolistic controls of the economy.... Most importantly, the bourgeoisie considered the tsarist regime responsible for the revolutionary crisis. In the end, however, it failed in its attempts to share power with tsarism so as to jointly head off the revolution.

Influential bourgeois circles had conceived of a little palace revolution with the aim of replacing the "unfit" tsar with another while preventing the interference of the masses. This required daring and determination, qualities which the Russian bourgeoisie did not possess. One should note that the bourgeoisie's conflict with tsarism and its oppositionist struggle contributed considerably to the weakening of tsarism, in part by isolating the latter among the propertied classes. In addition, the very course of events converted the bourgeoisie from opponents to supporters of the revolution.

The proletariat and peasantry were, as in 1905-1907, the fundamental revolutionary forces. They were the ones to launch "the movement of a revolutionary character for *bread, peace,* and *real liberty."* The urban industrial proletariat emerged, as in 1905, the initiator and leader of the revolution. It had freed itself from a certain innocence and faith in tsarist power acquired in 1905, and acted with determination and a desire to achieve liberty at any cost. The war hastened the political maturation of the peasantry by freeing it from many prejudices, first of all from monarchistic illusions. As far as the soldiers are concerned, most of whom were former peasants, they acquired in the midst of the harsh trials of war great political experience and became the leading and most organized part of the peasantry.

... What were the peculiarities of the actual course of the February Revolution? It was preceded by a powerful strike movement in the fall of 1916 and January-February, 1917. Similar to 1905, these strikes, both economic and political, acted as a major mobilizing factor and aroused the fighting spirit of fairly numerous proletarian masses. Their significance cannot be overstated. Without the massive political and economic strikes of February 23 and 24 — the very first days of the revolution — the bread riots, which served as the immediate cause of the revolutionary outbreak, would have turned into hunger riots and would have left no traces in history.

An important characteristic of the February events is their rapidity. This rapid tempo of the revolution is explainable by many reasons, which have yet to be fully analyzed by historians. Among these the first to be noted is the preservation of the revolutionary tradition of 1905, clearly evidenced by the fact that the active worker masses followed an acquired, classical pattern of action: from powerful strikes to general strike, from general strike to armed uprising. Further, the working class needed only four days to arouse, by its heroic example, the revolutionary enthusiasm of the soldiers caught up in the upheaval and to bring them into the uprising. There can be no doubt that the union of the worker and soldier uprising, one of the peculiarities of the February Revolution, ensured and hastened its triumph. The failure of this union in 1905-1907 was one of the reasons for the defeat of that revolution. Similarly, one can hardly doubt that without the leadership of the workers (in the person of Bolsheviks and progressive workers) over the rebellious soldiers the entry of the military in the February days would have taken on the character of an uncontrolled riot with all the accompanying consequences....

... The February Revolution, like the majority of authentic popular revolutions, developed as a spontaneous revolutionary upsurge. No one had organized and no one had foreseen (meaning the precise moment it would occur) the spontaneous revolutionary outbreak which occurred on February 23 and marked the beginning of the revolution. The Bolshevik cadres were trained, however, to be ready for any turn of events. The merit of the active centers of the Bolshevik party — the Russian Bureau of the Central Committee and the Petersburg committee of the Russian Social-Democratic Workers' party[5] — was to have immediately supported the massive action of the working men and women and to have done the maximum possible to lead the young movement and to guide it along organized lines. However, despite all the efforts of the Bolsheviks, the massive dimensions of the struggle and its rapid development outgrew the organizational possibilities of the small illegal party. Under those conditions the Petrograd organization could not bring under its leadership the growing revolutionary avalanche. Nonetheless, the revolutionary movement proceeded under the slogans and guiding ideological influence of the Bolshevik party. The worker masses acted in a rather organized and purposeful way in accord with the tactical line of the party. In a word, the proletarian and soldier masses behaved in their struggle with tsarism in a Bolshevik manner.

Thus, taken together, the gigantic preparatory work of the party readying the proletarian masses for the revolution and the truly dedicated activity of the Bolshevik organization of Petrograd at the moment of the decisive events made possible the transformation of a spontaneous mass outburst into a revolution.

However, one of the paradoxes of the February Revolution lies in the fact that these same masses, triumphant over tsarism and creators of the Soviets, allowed the Menshevik and SR leadership of the Petrograd Soviet to resolve the basic question of the revolution — state power — in a Menshevik manner. Here were apparent the insufficient numbers and, most importantly, the inadequate awareness and organizational unity of the broad proletarian masses. The aroused petty bourgeoisie, in the form of the soldiers, revealed their political inexperience and traditional faith in the upper bourgeoisie by swinging to its side and drew with them the majority of the proletariat. Here one must recognize the dialectics of real life,

---

5. Both committees located in the country's capital, Petrograd — Ed.

scarcely fitted to a simple schematic outline. The revolutionary proletariat was overwhelmed both intellectually and numerically by the petty bourgeoisie, whose views were expressed by the Mensheviks and SRs. In these conditions, the better organized liberal bourgeoisie had no difficulty seizing power from the revolutionary masses.

The bourgeoisie, seeing on February 27 that superiority of forces lay on the side of the revolution and that the tsarist government was in no condition to put down the "disorders," decided to join the revolution. It had no other choice since, having quarreled with the resolutely intransigent tsarist regime, it had no wish to tie its fate to the doomed tsarist counterrevolution. To a certain extent it felt as well the social-psychological effect created by the relatively easy triumph of the revolution. In addition, it saw that the revolution, which it had imagined a bloody riot, was not so terrible after all. It had every reason to expect that this revolution would turn out "glorious" and bloodless.... It should be emphasized that the bourgeoisie joined the revolution, thus becoming by necessity unexpected allies of the workers and peasants, in its concluding stages (February 27-March 2). As Lenin indicated, "By February 27 all classes joined together against the monarchy."

... Consequently, one of the peculiarities of this revolution was the fact that in the course of the February Revolution "there merged together in a remarkably 'friendly' manner, as a result of a very unique historical situation, *completely different* groups, *completely distinct* class interests, *completely contradictory* political and social aspirations." Lenin saw in this merging, in particular in the union of the bourgeoisie with the revolutionary class, one of the reasons for the relatively rapid and easy victory of the second Russian revolution. One should emphasize, however, that the merging of various forces and classes in the February days cannot be considered, to use contemporary terms, as a sort of united front of the proletariat, peasantry, and bourgeoisie.

When the affair was settled and the bourgeoisie was in the revolutionary camp, it pursued its own aims. It wanted, in the words of M. V. Rodzianko,[6] "to try to take over leadership and control of the movement to avoid ... anarchy." At the same time it devoted its efforts to saving the monarchy, since it needed a monarch as "the head of the bureaucracy and army for the defense of the privileges of capital against the laborers." Coming up against the opposition of the revolutionary masses, the bourgeoisie abandoned this goal. As a result, the February Revolution transformed the Russian bourgeoisie from monarchists to republicans.

The bourgeoisie was, however, successful in another matter — the struggle for state power, no longer against the fallen tsarist regime, now against the revolutionary masses who had established their revolutionary-democratic dictatorship in the form of the Petrograd Soviet. Disguising themselves as revolutionaries, lying, exploiting the traditional trust of the petty bourgeois masses in the bourgeoisie, taking advantage of the petty bourgeois cowardliness of the Menshevik-SR leaders of the Petrograd Soviet, the bourgeois Duma leaders were able to seize state power from the hands of the people. The Mensheviks and SR's, whose supporters controlled the Soviet, frightened by the scope of the revolution and faithful to their dogma about the leading role of the bourgeoisie in a bourgeois revolution, incited the Soviet to transfer power voluntarily to the bourgeoisie.

Nonetheless, the workers and soldiers, in part consciously and in part instinctively, did not allow full powers to be concentrated in the hands of the bourgeois Provisional Government. Relying on the armed masses, the Soviets in fact possessed all the attributes of real power. Therefore, there appeared in the country an extremely original and contradictory merger of two authorities, of two dictatorships — the bourgeoisie in the form of the Provisional Government, and the proletarian-peasant revolutionary-democratic dictatorship in the form of the Soviets. V. I.

6. One of Russia's leading conservatives and President of the last Duma — Ed.

Lenin explained this outcome of the February Revolution, termed dual power, by the fact that this was no ordinary bourgeois revolution, that it closely resembled a revolutionary-democratic revolution. Dual power describes well the remarkable originality of the February Revolution. The revolution also departed from the bourgeois model in the social sphere (the appearance of worker control[7]). The revolutionary conquests of the proletarian and democratic masses in local areas were particularly great.

The fundamental reason for such an outcome of the February Revolution was the fact that the new historical epoch of imperialism and world war brought much closer together the bourgeois-democratic and socialist stages of the revolution in Russia. Therefore, V. I. Lenin considered the February Revolution as the first, opening stage of the Russian Revolution. He was not only convinced that it would evolve into a socialist revolution, but also elaborated an objectively correct, concrete plan for the transition from the first stage of the revolution to the second. He considered the Soviets, led by the revolutionary proletariat, to be the political motor for this evolution and powerful monopolistic capitalism to provide its material prerequisites. Taking into account the backwardness and interdependence of the economy of the country, Lenin proposed to achieve the transformation to socialism, not immediately or directly, but by means of a series of transitional means and steps.

... One of the most notable results of Lenin's analysis of the February Revolution is his conclusion that the newly empowered bourgeoisie could not solve the gigantic tasks presented by the revolution. It was impossible to give the masses peace, bread, and complete freedom "without abandoning the framework of bourgeois relations." These broadly democratic tasks were so transformed in the period of imperialism that they took on an anticapitalist character. The bourgeoisie was thus incapable of accomplishing them, for this was something only the revolutionary proletariat could do....

Thus the February Revolution in all respects confirmed, as Lenin emphasized, the correctness of Bolsehvik ideas and slogans for the period of the bourgeois-democratic revolution. In conformity with the Bolshevik, Leninist conception of the revolution, the proletariat became its initiator and leader. It attracted to its side in the course of the revolution the progressive peasantry — the soldiers. This revolutionary alliance of the proletariat and the peasantry destroyed the tsarist regime and assured victory. Consequently, the Leninist idea of the alliance of these two classes was proven correct by history.

An armed uprising, as the Bolsheviks had already declared, proved to be the sole means to overthrow tsarism. Having achieved victory, the workers and soldiers created their own organ of revolutionary power, the Soviets. We should note here that the appearance of the Soviets was an indication of the deep crisis of bourgeois democracy in Russia and of the birth of a new, proletarian democracy.

However, in Lenin's words, "no one could foresee" the further evolution of the revolution — the bourgeoisie, opponent of the revolution, became its supporter, and the Soviets voluntarily handed over power to the Provisional Government; instead of unified power there appeared dual power, never before seen in world history. As a result, it became necessary in October, 1917 to overthrow by force the bourgeois dictatorship, in place of a peaceful transition from the revolutionary-democratic dictatorship of the proletariat and peasantry to a socialist dictatorship of the proletariat, as had been anticipated by Bolshevik theories of 1905.... Lenin had expressed his forceful opposition in the war years to a bloc with the revolutionary chauvinists. Though the leaders of the party had maintained this position, things turned out differently in the conditions of mass struggle. In the February days a temporary bloc was formed spontaneously, from below, between prole-

---

7. The efforts of factory workers to influence the conduct of affairs, even at times to take over control of their factories — Ed.

tarian-internationalist and defensist elements.[8] One cannot overlook this fact as one of the reasons why the revolution, directed against the war, quickly adopted the position of revolutionary defensism.

8. The term "defensist elements" refers to those groups among the radical parties who supported the war to assure the defense of Russia (and indirectly of the Western democracies); hence the policy they backed was known as "revolutionary defensism" – Ed.

Thus the logical development of the revolution, when placed in the concrete historical circumstances of Russia in the early twentieth century, acquired a special form in the February Revolution, the first triumphant bourgeois-democratic revolution in the period of imperialism. The February Revolution completed the bourgeois-democratic stage in the revolutionary liberation movement in our country.

## *William G. Rosenberg*

# THE INSTABILITY OF LIBERAL GOVERNMENT

The party which defended the interests of those groups Volobuev calls the "liberal bourgeoisie" was the Constitutional Democratic (Cadet) party. Its leaders in Petrograd, many of whom were well known as liberal opponents of the tsarist regime in the Duma, emerged in the first days of the revolution as key figures in the creation of a new government. What aims did this party pursue, and how capable was it of implementing these goals? William Rosenberg (1938- ), professor of history at the University of Michigan, argues that its leadership sought a new government which would receive the support of the nation, a goal that they had tried and failed to achieve in the Duma. Their objectives were shaped in his opinion by their liberal political philosophy and the needs of the war, not by class interests as Volobuev maintains. The excerpt presented here begins on February 27, a day of massive demonstrations and mutiny in the Petrograd garrison.

WHILE Kadets and their Duma colleagues debated, however, events were moving rapidly. Revolutions leave little time for reticence. By early afternoon on the 27th Petrograd was again filled with demonstrators. Word came of the first garrison defections; shortly afterward, shots could be heard even from inside the Duma chambers. Meanwhile, a revolutionary council of workers' and soldiers' representatives, the Petrograd Soviet, was organizing in rooms adjacent to the Duma's in the Tauride Palace, modeling its actions on the famous revolutionary Soviet of 1905. While there is little in the surviving sources to indicate exactly how delegates to the new organization were elected, scores of noisy and enthusiastic representatives began streaming to the

Selections from William G. Rosenberg, *Liberals in the Russian Revolution: The Constitutional Democratic Party, 1917-1921*, pp. 51-58, 70-74. Copyright © 1974 by Princeton University Press. Reprinted by permission of Princeton University Press.

Tauride from all parts of the city, soldiers bursting in with news of more troops "joining the people against the cursed autocracy," socialist intellectuals jubilantly swearing "to serve the people's cause to the last drop of blood." As it seemed about to take full control of the situation, the Soviet's whole mood and atmosphere created an almost irresistible — one might almost say physical — pressure to take action.

This pressure culminated, finally, in the behavior of rebellious troops themselves, many of whom soon began pledging their "full support and loyalty" not only to the Soviet, but also to the Duma. Few in the Duma leadership group had any desire for martyrdom, either in the cause of authority or on the barricades of revolution; and the fact that tank-and-file soldiers turned to them enthusiastically surprised a number of Kadets and their colleagues alike. But because they did, Duma leaders were implicated in the rebellion whether they wanted to be or not. And under these pressures, the "private conference" of Duma representatives finally directed its Council of Elders to act.[1]

Late in the evening on the 27th, a special "Temporary Duma Committee" declared itself in power. Its members included Miliukov and Nekrasov from among the Kadets, and its official title was "Committee of State Representatives for the Reestablishment of Order in the Capital and for Relations with Persons and Institutions," as cautious and reluctant an appellation as ever assumed by any revolutionary body. Willingly or not, the Committee declared its intention of "forming a new government corresponding to the desires of the population and capable of commanding its confidence." And it appealed to the city for calm.

The formation of the Temporary Duma Committee brought the question of state power into clear focus. Was the new regime to reflect the mood and aspiration of Petrograd workers and soldiers, to seek social as well as political transformation, and to be revolutionary in fact as well as in name? Or was it to carry on the basic tasks of its tsarist predecessor, only with more efficiency and, presumably, more success?

From the Petrograd Kadets' perspective, three closely related goals had to be met, all of which, on inspection, can be seen as designed to consolidate and control Russia's "revolutionary situation," rather than extend it: the end of mass unrest and the restoration of order in Petrograd; support from the army and the avoidance at all costs of civil war; and the implementation of those reforms which were capable of resolving Russia's general administrative and economic crisis. Most Kadets thus believed the alternatives for a new regime were limited. The capability to end mass unrest required a government which masses of dissident workers and soldiers felt would to some extent represent their interests. This clearly ruled out a military regime, a government of the right, or even a liberal dictatorship. The need for the army's support meant that the new regime had to maintain reasonably close ties with the old order, particularly on the question of Russia's commitments in the war, which limited its radicalism. Finally, the satisfaction of complex supply and distribution problems meant enlisting the support both of qualified administrative personnel and Russia's industrial bourgeoisie, whose managerial and technical expertise was essential to economic efficiency. In particular, practical competence would have to be assured if Russia was now to devote her full resources to defeating the Germans, the principal grounds on which most in the Duma justified their participation in the rebellion. This meant that, at its core, the new regime had to be liberal or at least nonpartisan, which of course corresponded to the Kadets' own theoretical orientation.

For most Central Committee members in Petrograd, the logical course in these circumstances was to invest full power in the Duma (and thus Miliukov's Progressive Bloc

---

1. The "private conference" brought together the Duma representatives whom the tsar had just tried to disband by a prorogation decree, and whose elected leaders were the Council of Elders — Ed.

coalition,[2] which many assumed the Kadet leader could control). Though elected on a limited franchise, Russia's parliament still represented a number of the country's most talented political leaders, particularly from among the Kadets, whose influence was far greater than their numerical strength. It was also a bulwark against any move on the city by the army's high command. Its leaders had worked closely with the general staff in the past, and it represented institutional continuity with the old regime. Who could accuse Russia's entire national parliament of sedition?

Whether the monarchy should be preserved, provided the Duma created a new "responsible ministry," was apparently of little concern. Right Kadets like the staid academician S. F. Oldenburg thought it should, but the Central Committee as a whole inclined to the opinion that the "monarchy factually did not exist," and that it was "undesirable and pointless to fight for its resurrection." Consequently, while Miliukov and Nekrasov sat with the Temporary Duma Committee in the Tauride Palace, the Central Committee itself sent representatives throughout the city to address troop units and help take control of state institutions in the Duma's name. Paul Gronskii "seized" the telegraph agency; Vasili Maklakov and Moisei Adzhemov "secured" the Ministry of Justice; Victor Pepeliaev, Ivan Demidov, and Vasili Stepanov set out for Tsarskoe Selo and Kronstadt to establish contact with their garrisons. While those in the streets shouted "Down with Nicholas!" the slogan of the Kadet Central Committee was "Long Live the Duma!"

This outlook coincided neatly with that of many members of the Duma itself, particularly its ambitious president, Nicholas Rodzianko. For most of February 28, Rodzianko spent his time cultivating support for a cabinet responsible to the Duma, headed by himself. Apparently he was persuasive. A number of generals were soon convinced that, while the Petrograd situation was potentially catastrophic for the war effort, a Duma with full powers had a good chance of bringing it under control. From staff headquarters in Mogilev on March 1, General Alekseev[3] sent the tsar an urgent telegram, insisting that the Duma be supported. He also requested the appointment of a responsible ministry, with Rodzianko as prime minister. Other army leaders cabled similar views, while General N. V. Ruzskii, an aide-de-camp, stood by in Pskov to argue in person. Rodzianko, meanwhile, also planned to meet Nicholas in Pskov, expecting that the tsar would confirm both his own appointment as premier and the ministerial reform. When Nicholas and his entourage arrived late in the afternoon of March 1, General Ruzskii met him before dinner. The two talked for most of the evening. Around 11 p.m., Alekseev's telegram arrived, apparently ending any argument. Ruzskii then communicated with Rodzianko by telegraph, reporting the tsar's consent to a responsible ministry. He also indicated that a manifesto to this effect had been drafted.

Meanwhile, Miliukov and other members of the Temporary Duma Committee were negotiating in the Tauride Palace with representatives of the Petrograd Soviet. Regarded by the left as the "spirit and backbone" of liberal Russia and "'boss' of all bourgeois elements," the Kadet leader himself was a focal point of these talks, independently of his party's Central Committee. His principal concern was to create a strong but nonpartisan national regime, capable of preserving Russia's national interests rather than satisfying class demands or implementing social reforms. Insofar as a revolution could be supported in wartime, it was only as a means of rationalizing the country's state structure to further the military effort. This required an authoritative government of statesmen, not of bickering politicians.

The crucial consideration for Miliukov was the establishment of firm state authority, which seemed to depend on two factors: support from the Soviet, whose leaders

---

2. The Progressive Bloc was formed in 1915 as a means of increasing the Duma's political influence — Ed.

3. Commander-in-chief of the Russian army — Ed.

clearly exercised whatever control there was over rebellious Petrograd; and sanction from existing state authority, namely the tsar, whose endorsement was necessary to invest the new government with "legal" power and to secure the support of the army. With these concerns in mind, Miliukov quickly came to the conclusion, in contrast to his colleagues on the Kadet Central Committee, that the Duma could not become the basis for a responsible government under Rodzianko. The evidence here is hard to sort out. There is some indication that Miliukov had actually lost faith in a political role for the Duma some months before, despite his continued efforts on behalf of the Progressive Bloc. But it also seems apparent that pressure from the Soviet pushed him in this direction. In any event, the main consideration for Miliukov was the fact that the Duma was not democratically elected, but class-based, and never regarded by the left as a true national parliament. In the context of revolutionary democracy, with the broadest possible extension of political freedom and civil liberties, it was hardly likely that a cabinet responsible to its propertied ... delegates could long maintain popular support. The sources do not say so directly, but Miliukov most likely felt that *any* form of direct accountability was inappropriate for Russia in the context of revolution. With their own limited national constituency, the Kadets themselves could never claim the right to rule on the basis of representative principles; and politically inexperienced Russian workers and peasants were not accustomed to representational authority. No effective policies, moreover, were likely to be implemented if ministers were more interested in currying popular favor than in taking decisive, necessary action; the task of the new regime had to be national, not sectarian.

We do know, moreover, that Miliukov felt the Duma had lost its political initiative by obeying the prorogation decree on the 27th. "Legally," it now had no more claim to power than any other ad hoc group, such as the Petrograd Soviet. In retrospect, it is clear that Soviet leaders had no intention of taking state power, fearing this would provoke a ruthless counterrevolution, and reinforced by Marxist convictions which postulated a clearly defined bourgeois stage of development before Russia could move toward socialism. But in the hours of frenzied activity at the Tauride Palace, the left's possible political aspirations greatly concerned the tiring Miliukov. The only acceptable course, considering all factors, was a totally new regime, not based on the Duma, but independently vested with "the plenitude of power."

The crucial element in Miliukov's vision, however, was the sanction of the tsar. Unless the monarchy continued to exist in some form to endorse a new government, preferably as a regency under Grand Duke Michael, Miliukov felt that neither the army command and conservative, upper-class Russia on one hand, nor the untutored mass of workers, peasants, and soldiers on the other, would recognize its authority. Soviet leaders negotiating with the Temporary Duma Committee felt Miliukov's concern was "utopian" in view of the "general hatred of the monarchy among the masses of the people," but were not prepared to make the question a major issue. The monarchy was simply not "an important factor"; in any event, a constituent assembly would certainly establish a republic in the not-too-distant future. What was a factor, however, was the possibility of counterrevolution. Already by February 28 there were rumors of loyalist troops moving on the capital under General Ivanov.[4] In dealing with this problem, a number of leftists thought the monarchy could prove useful.

Thus the liberal plan for a responsible ministry collapsed as Miliukov, the country's leading Kadet and ostensible "boss" of right-wing Russia, negotiated a provisional government committed to political freedom and a constituent assembly, but sanctioned by a figurehead regent rather than the Duma. While obviously not the only member of the Temporary Duma Committee to take

---

4. Commander of the Petrograd garrison — Ed.

this position, Miliukov was clearly most influential. It is not too much to say that largely as a result of his efforts, the dejected Rodzianko was forced to wire General Ruzskii in the early hours of March 2 that the tsar's manifesto in favor of a responsible ministry was not too late.

Meanwhile, such was Miliukov's position of authority in the Tauride Palace that he himself wrote part of the Soviet's declaration supporting the new government on March 2 (in which, according to Sergei Melgunov, it was he who included the phrase that Russia was "not yet free from the dangers of military movement against the revolution"). And such was his self-assurance that, even before the delegates to Pskov brought back the tsar's sanction for an independent, provisional regime, Miliukov stood in the Ekaterinskii Hall of the Tauride Palace, in one of the most famous incidents of the March period, and declared to an assembled throng that a new government "elected by the revolution" would govern under the regency of Grand Duke Michael.

This particular speech would haunt the Kadet leader the rest of his life. While shrewd in calculating the monarchy's possible role in consolidating state authority in the face of right-wing opposition, Miliukov badly misjudged the temper of Petrograd. Instantly, on hearing the word "regency," the crowd at the Tauride roared its disapproval. ("Prolonged bursts of indignation," the transcript in *Isvestiia* reads; "Exclamation: 'Long Live the Republic!' 'Down with the Dynasty!'") Moreover, Miliukov also overestimated the popularity of his scheme with the new members of the government, and even with Grand Duke Michael himself. On the morning of March 3, in a dramatic confrontation at the Grand Duke's apartment on Millionnaia Street, Miliukov found hilself practically alone in arguing the necessity of monarchic symbolism. Michael refused to accept the crown without much hesitation. The monarchy dissolved, with the Kadet leader himself one of its last prominent defenders.

For the Kadet party as a whole, the political implications of Miliukov's actions were quickly apparent. From the left came charges of counterrevolution, of upholding the standards of reaction; on the right there was hostility over the collapse of Rodzianko's plan for a ministry responsible to the conservative Duma. Neither development could help the Kadets broaden their base of support, a necessary step if the party was to develop its strength in the forthcoming period of electoral democracy. Late on the afternoon of March 3, in fact, Miliukov determined to withdraw completely from government affairs, having earlier stated that the perpetuation of the monarchy was a condition for his accepting a ministerial position. Only a special delegation from the Kadet Central Committee, led by Vinaver and Babokov, persuaded him to change his mind.

Even within the Central Committee, there was much consternation over Miliukov's independent actions. Nekrasov was particularly bitter, having hoped the Kadets would help the abdication go smoothly; others felt divisions among Kadets were deepened when they should have been healed. More important, there were fears that doubts would now develop among workers and soldiers about the orientation of the new provisional cabinet itself.

Though hardly a Kadet creation alone, the new regime was composed almost entirely of liberal figures. It sprang from the Progressive Bloc, which had been working on the composition of a possible liberal ministry since the summer of 1915 when it first proposed the famous "Cabinet of Defense." Its head was Prince George Lvov, a nonparty zemstvo leader[5] chosen more for his disassociation from politics than for political skills, and largely at the urging of Miliukov, who wanted to be sure the new cabinet had little direct connection with the Fourth Duma. But the Kadet leader himself, who took the post of minister of foreign affairs, was clearly its dominant personality; and his closest associates from the Petrograd party group held important posts.... While the socialist Alexander Kerensky also joined the

---

5. The *zemstva* were regional representative assemblies charged with local affairs — Ed.

cabinet, and Nicholas Nekrasov, the new Kadet minister of transport, was generally considered a radical, the remaining ministers were all likely to support Kadet party views.... Thus the regime was as much a Kadet government as party leaders could reasonably expect, though the party's Central Committee played no direct role in its formation, and some have even argued that masonry was a more important factor than politics in structuring its composition.[6]

What this would mean in terms of the government's programs and policies remained to be seen. Reflecting the Petrograd Kadet ethos, the new provisional regime was decidedly "nonpartisan" in all of its initial pronouncements, officially committing itself to national rather than sectarian interests. But it was hardly representative. Instead it reflected the emphasis on elite rather than mass politics which had characterized the approach of Petrograd Kadets generally (and which Miliukov himself may have felt was a necessary means of circumventing the political implications of the liberals' own narrow electoral base); it was concerned with political, not social democracy; and it reflected the intense desire to win the war and advance Russia's "national interests" which had largely impelled all of the Kadets' own policies in the preceding two and one-half years....

The problem most concerning Miliukov and his fellow ministers in the first days of March ... was ... the new government's authority. In effect, the regime had unilaterally declared itself in power. Though supported by the Petrograd Soviet, itself an ad hoc body, its legitimacy was tenuous; and unless the liberal ministers had effective power, it was unlikely that Russia's other problems could be solved.

The most obvious means of securing the nation's confidence, once Miliukov's plan of obtaining monarchic sanction had failed, was to stress a commitment to the rapid convocation of a democratically elected constituent (or constitutional) assembly. This became the government's "primary duty" according to its general declaration of March 6, equaled in importance only by national defense. Yet for several reasons, Miliukov and his liberal colleagues had reservations about convening the assembly. One was the difficulty of holding fully democratic elections in the midst of a war, with millions in the fluid status of military service, and millions more completely ignorant of even the most basic democratic political processes. As we have seen, Miliukov and other Kadet party leaders, particularly in Petrograd, had come to assume a long period of political evolution before Russia was fully ready for representative democracy, despite the commitments of the Kadet party program; Miliukov's own goal in 1916 had been a liberal dictatorship on the model of Lloyd George's cabinet in England or Clemenceau's in France, at least until the end of the war. Also, Russia's pressing economic and social problems could simply not wait until the country was organized for national elections. However unpopular they might be to different groups of the population, measures had to be taken by the provisional regime at once, particularly to support the army. Finally, there was the probability that any national election campaign would intensify partisanship in Russia, increasing social polarization perhaps even to the point of civil war, as class-oriented parties fought for support of their programs; at the very least, a campaign might undermine what Kadets saw as Russia's "national concensus," whose development and maintenance was necessary for military victory.

In effect, therefore, while proclaiming their democratic commitments, Russia's new liberal ministers had no intention of foregoing the "right" to address themselves to pressing national problems even before any elections were held; and implicitly, this meant the necessity of defining "acceptable limits" to revolutionary change, at least for the time being. Indeed, leaving aside any

---

6. Many of its members belonged to the fraternal order of Free Masons — Ed.

7. Lloyd George and Clemenceau set up strong governments for the pursuit of the war against Germany — Ed.

question of the Kadets' own class interests (which one might well argue would benefit from the postponement of many of the reforms being advocated by socialist radicals), it is difficult to see how they could have done otherwise, given the nation's needs and the lack of any established mechanism for effective democratic representation. Yet the revolution had been carried to fruition by a flood of mass frustration and hostility, which the new ministers could easily find turned against themselves. Also, unless new policies reflected mass aspirations, the new regime would have to enforce its decisions with the same coercive measures used by the tsarist autocracy, which again might easily lead to civil war.

The existence of the Petrograd Soviet posed special problems in this regard. Ostensibly a representative body itself, whose policies were to reflect the interests of Russia's workers, peasants, and soldiers, the Soviet clearly rivaled the government as an institution of authority. Moreover, other local soviets, modeling themselves on the Petrograd example, were springing up in virtually every significant city and town. By the end of March, they existed in more than 70 localities in the central region alone; and in the Ural industrial region, there were more than 100. Peasant soviets were also organizing in the countryside, although in some places news of the revolution itself did not arrive for several weeks. These groups raised obvious questions about the comprehensiveness of the government's own power — the specter of *dvoevlastie*, or dual authority, as Miliukov and others described it.

The Petrograd Kadet leadership worried about "dual authority" from the first days of the revolution, arguing that whatever the new form of political control in Russia, authority could not be held effectively by more than one institution. What bothered Miliukov and his colleagues most was the soviets' obvious partisanship, at odds with their own hope of maintaining a sentiment of national unity. They also worried that "blinded radicals" might use the new organizations to launch a coup d'état in the future.

Yet it was also clear that for the time being, at least, the new regime *needed* the power exercised by the soviets. When Demidov, Stepanov, Rodichev, Gronskii, and other Kadets went out to enlist the support of army garrisons in the first days of March, for example, they leaned heavily on Petrograd Soviet spokesmen who accompanied them for support and protection. Also, Soviet and Duma Committee proclamations were co-authored on several occasions; their military commissions were joined; and at one point Miliukov himself even insisted that published statements from both groups be printed together "to underscore their mutual relationship." It was also Miliukov who insisted, along with other Kadets in Petrograd, that the Soviet leadership use its influence to prevent further demonstrations by workers. He also regarded it as the Soviet's obligation to restore and maintain civil order, assuring at the same time — since the socialists controlled the printers' union — that all parties, including those on the right, enjoyed freedom of the press and other civil liberties.

The local soviets were also important to the government in terms of the army and the front. More than 7 million front-echelon soldiers, stretched along a 3,000 kilometer line from the Baltic to the Black Sea, hoped at the very least that the revolution would bring some relief from the hardships of discipline and short supplies. Any effective military posture required that the troops remain orderly. But in some places, soldiers were reacting to the news from Petrograd with an enthusiasm bordering on anarchy; and elsewhere, officers hostile to the revolution (or in some cases, those with German names), were wantonly shot. On March 2, moreover, a group of radical leftists published the famous Order Number 1,[8] which not only freed soldiers from the humiliating rigors of tsarist military discipline, but also ordered the creation of soldiers' committees to direct and oversee each unit. At once scores of units both in Petrograd and at the front began to look to the Petrograd Soviet

---

8. First order issued by the Petrograd Soviet — Ed.

as their source of authority, rather than to the government.

Kadets in Petrograd vigorously protested Order Number 1, but even before its publication, implicitly recognized Soviet power in the question of military discipline. On March 1 and 2, when Miliukov and other liberals were concerned that the Petrograd garrison could not defend the revolution if loyalist troops counterattacked, they relied on the Soviet to bring officers and men together and restore the garrison's fighting capabilities. Similarly, when it appeared that scores of army units were stretching Order Number 1 (which supposedly applied only to the Petrograd garrison), and were electing their officers in total disregard for the traditional chain of command, it was the Soviet which was expected to bring them to their senses.

Several left Kadets, particularly Nicholas Nekrasov, argued in the beginning of March that the network of soviets offered a temporary solution to the problem of government accountability. The authority exercised by these "unofficial" organs did not so much overlap the government's as run in parallel lines, with the composition of the provisional ministry reflecting Russia's professional classes, public organizations, bourgeoisie, and army officers; and that of the soviets representing millions of workers, peasants, and soldiers, particularly those in Moscow and Petrograd, and at the front. Until the convening of the Constituent Assembly, liberal ministers could "legitimize" their power by tailoring decisions to the soviets' wishes.

But just as Miliukov and his supporters worried about a revolutionary cabinet responsible to the old Fourth Duma, they were equally adamant about the government's independence from the soviets. Accountability to one partisan group raised the problem of support from others; and if mass popularity became the basis for political power before the Constituent Assembly, the position of the Kadets themselves, judging by past Duma elections, was likely to become even more tenuous than it already was. In a context of revolutionary change, moreover, an independent government of "national," "nonpartisan" liberals was far better able, in Miliukov's view, to determine what was truly in Russia's national interest than organizations which themselves were formed on an ad hoc basis. Consequently, Miliukov and his liberal colleagues insisted that the power of the new regime could not in any way be circumscribed. They took their posts instead as if they were a "ministry of confidence" under the old regime, warning the soviets not to encroach on their "legitimate authority."

In these circumstances, if the liberal ministers used their self-proclaimed legitimacy to introduce policies at variance with the desires of workers, peasants, and soldiers, as expressed through the soviets, it would only be a matter of time before Russia faced a new political crisis. And given the dual nature of power which existed in fact, as well as Russia's enormous practical needs, even minor disagreements were bound to have a serious effect on the political and social stability most Kadets so much desired.

*Oskar Anweiler*

# THE IDEALS OF REVOLUTIONARY DEMOCRACY

The Petrograd Soviet appeared even before the Provisional Government. Its membership was made up of hundreds of delegates from the city's factories, more still from the regiments of the garrison. Its leadership was composed from the start, however, of radical intellectuals belonging largely to the Menshevik and SR parties. What goals did they seek and why did they choose to back the Provisional Government? Oskar Anweiler (1925- ), professor of history at Ruhr University, Bochum, Germany, emphasizes on the one hand their commitment to "revolutionary self-government" and on the other their concern with "practical considerations" of government.

THE RUSSIAN Revolution of 1917 has its victors, whose heirs still rule the country. It has its victims too, but fifty years after the event, their names survive mostly in archives. The historiography of the Russian Revolution is devoted, in the main, to the leading figures of the victorious party and to their actions, while the defeated have been swept away into the "dustbin of history" as Trotsky had prophesied on the night of the victorious October insurrection. The power of these political dreamers, it has been often said, ran through their fingers like water. They have been called prisoners of their own fictitious ideology, men who did not understand the signs of the times. The representatives of "Socialist Democracy" — Tseretelli, Martov, Chernov, or Avksentiev,[1] appear at best as champions of high ideals, as honest and sincere socialists, but also as men unwilling to strive for power and to use it unscrupulously. They stood in direct contract to the two stars of October, Lenin and Trotsky, who subjected the social dynamics of the revolution to their political calculations. The usual judgment of historians is that the inevitability of the Bolshevik victory resulted from the failure of the democratic forces, and that this failure in turn derived from their political ideas, which, applied to Russia of 1917, proved illusory.

The critical attention of historians has been mainly directed at the politics of the socialist parties who from the February Revolution until autumn enjoyed a majority in the different public organizations and institutions; that is, the Socialist Revolutionaries and the Mensheviks who claimed to embody the "revolutionary democracy" as opposed to the "bourgeois democracy" of the liberals. This socialist center, which viewed itself as the left, has been put on trial by two different historical prosecutors. It has been blamed for lack of revolutionary energy and radical decisiveness, for example by O. H. Radkey, who demonstrates with grim pleasure and in precise detail all the mistakes and errors of the Socialist Revolutionary Party. Or, on the contrary, it has been accused by Miliukov and the liberal-conservative Russian émigré writers of clinging to a particular class interest instead of showing readiness to assume all-Russian responsibility. The difference in expectations — already evidenced in 1917 — toward the policies of the Soviet majority on the part of the Bolsheviks and the Liberals then revealed

---

1. Tseretelli and Martov were Mensheviks, Chernov and Avksentiev Socialist Revolutionaries – Ed.

From Oskar Anweiler, "The Political Ideology of the Leaders of the Petrograd Soviet in the Spring of 1917," in Richard Pipes (ed.), *Revolutionary Russia* (Cambridge, Mass., 1968), pp. 114-125.

that "dilemma of ideas within the struggle for power" which afterwards resounds time and again in the memoirs of a Chernov or a Tseretelli.

It is the purpose of this paper to analyze the political ideas of the leaders of the "revolutionary democracy," that is, the leaders of the Soviet majority, in the first months of the revolution, insofar as they concern the vital question of state power and the establishment of a new political order in Russia.

The ideological dilemma of the majority parties in the spring of 1917 originated in the tension between former political goals, as laid down in doctrines at the beginning of the century and during the Revoltuion of 1905, and the new revolutionary situation. The crisis that resulted from this confrontation was resolved with the entrance of the socialist representatives into the Provisional Government[2] — a process accompanied as well as impeded by a simultaneous confrontation with a new state model, the Soviet Republic, proclaimed by Lenin. Because in the spring and summer of 1917 the moderate Socialist parties had their political basis in the Soviets of Workers', Soldiers', and Peasants' Deputies, they suddenly found themselves closely bound to the existence and destiny of the soviets, although the soviets had previously assumed no importance either in their political programs or their concepts of the future state and society. Until October 1917, the non-Bolshevik socialists had not clarified their position toward the soviets; their factional splits revealed trends leading in divergent directions.

In general, the origin and the political structure of the Soviets of Workers' and Soldiers' Deputies of 1917 and, to a lesser degree, of the Soviets of the Peasants' Deputies are known, although some aspects still require research. Among the soviets, the Petrograd Soviet was virtually alone to function as a political organ of countrywide importance, at least up to the time of the First All Russian Conference (March 29 to April 3) and the First All-Russian Congress of Workers' and Soldiers' Soviets (June 3-24). But even after the formation of all-Russian central soviet organs, the Petrograd Soviet maintained in effect the political predominance established in the first days of the revolution. This fact proved later to be decisive for the victory of the Bolsheviks in execution of the October insurrection.

The initial stage in the development of the Petrograd Soviet extends from the period of the first meeting of the "Provisional Executive Committee" in the afternoon of February 27 to the formation of the first coalition cabinet on May 5. During these two months the Petrograd Soviet not only developed and consolidated its structure, but acquired new political self-confidence as an organ of political control that the "revolutionary democracy" exercised over the government.

Before proceeding to analyze the political ideology of the Petrograd Soviet in March-April 1917, we must sketch its political and social profile. Unfortunately, the sources at our disposal are not as abundant as they should be for a precise sociological analysis (a statement that might also be applied to the history of the soviet movement as a whole).

The representation ratio for the election of the deputies until the electoral readjustment of mid-April, gave a certain preference to the soldiers, who therefore enjoyed a majority in the plenary meetings. Among the workers, deputies of the big factories were at a numerical disadvantage compared to those of the smaller ones. Thus, the social physiognomy of the Petrograd Soviet in the first period was not predominantly proletarian in the Marxist sense, but rather peasant and petty bourgeois (because a relatively high proportion of the soldiers' deputies came from the middle ranks and had a higher education). Trotsky saw in this fact the main reason for the initial preponderance of the Socialist Revolutionaries in the Petrograd Soviet.

More important for the political function of the Soviet, however, was the fact that from the very beginning the control was

---

2. In May — Ed.

mainly in the hands of socialist intellectuals who, as Trotsky again rightly maintained, created a sort of "reserve and shadow government." Toward the end of March, only seven of the 42 members of the Executive Committee were workers. Besides such journalists as Sukhanov and Steklov, the Committee was dominated by socialist Duma deputies, as, for example, Chkheidze, Skobelev, and (after March 19) Tseretelli.

The predominance of intellectuals differentiated the 1917 Petrograd Soviet from its predecessor of 1905. The latter had originated as a strike committee and therefore never lost its character as an organ of worker "self-government." In 1917, by contrast, the structure of political parties, emerging from illegal or semi-legal status, with their theoretical, tactical, and personal contradictions, overlapped with the fundamentally different structure of the soviets. The "pure" soviet principle, which Hannah Arendt has recently depicted as the antithesis of the party system, existed only in the first elections to the Petrograd Soviet; the factions in the soviet constituted themselves along party lines. Political party leaders like Lenin, Trotsky, Chernov, and others managed immediately on their arrival from the emigration to secure a seat in the soviet. Before 1917, the conflict among the socialists in Russia had taken place less in the Duma than in the underground. Now it was brought into the open, into the arena of the Soviet.

This crystallization of the Soviet along party lines occurred already in March 1917. The process is interesting because it is symptomatic of the transformation of the soviets from a supra-party, revolutionary organ into a semi-parliamentary deputation of workers and the garrison, a body that embraced the entire spectrum of Russian socialism and its parties. By the end of March, all Russian and non-Russian socialist parties and groups of any importance were represented in the Executive Committee of the soviet, alongside trade union representatives, whether with a voting or merely a consultative vote. For the participants as well as for the non-socialist public at large, the whole embodied "revolutionary democracy." In the provincial soviets this process of crystallization along party lines took longer than in the capital cities of Petrograd and Moscow. In some localities, the political physiognomy of the soviets remained unclear even in the summer and autumn of 1917, not the least because at the beginning the contrasts between the local Bolshevik organizations and the other socialist parties were less pronounced.

All the socialist parties (in contrast to the anarchists) regarded the soviets as an organizing machinery for the activation and articulation of the political consciousness of the toiling masses in accord with their revolutionary party programs. This attitude led to fundamental difficulties: the tendency to organize and lead from "above" ran into the opposite pressure from "below." In the eyes of the soldiers and workers who were about to be organized by the parties assisted by the soviets, these improvised institutions of direct democracy were in most cases not substitutes for parliaments but rather revolutionary clubs and permanent assemblies of the revolutionary masses. The revolutionary *stikhiia*[3] in the soviets and soviet-like committees was always on the alert. Already, during the April demonstrations in Petrograd one could observe an estrangement between the leadership of the Petrograd Soviet and parts of the working class and the garrison, both of which followed more radical slogans and sought to exert pressure on the Executive Committee of the Soviet. The quick settlement of the dispute, however, demonstrated that the authority of the soviet leadership was as yet unshaken.

In the early summer of 1917, the spread of Factory Councils[4] ... produced in the form of the Central Council of the Petrograd Factory Committees, a political organ competing with the Petrograd Soviet. The Bolsheviks held in it a preponderance from the

---

3. *Stikhiia* is best translated here as "popular revolutionary forces" — Ed.
4. Factory Councils were elected by workers in their factories to assert their right to share in the management of the enterprise — Ed.

very outset. There was no fixed delimitation of functions between the Soviet and the Central Council of the Factory Committees, even though the former concerned itself mainly with political problems and the latter with questions of economics and internal factory issues. Because they served the worker directly at his working place, their revolutionary influence increased in proportion as the Soviet became a permanent institution and lost close contact with the masses. In the eyes of the non-Bolshevik majority of the Soviet, the instability of the Factory Councils — their membership was undergoing constant change — demonstrated the lack of maturity of the Russian working class, its unpreparedness for "a dictatorship of the proletariat." For the Bolsheviks, on the contrary, it served as the basis of agitation. It was Lenin's and Trotsky's masterly tactic to connect their political program, aimed at taming and leading the revolutionary masses, with the *stikhiia* latent in the soviets and incited by the Bolsheviks since the spring of 1917, and in this manner to seize power. One might say that on the eve of October, the Bolsheviks retransformed the soviets from semiparliamentary institutions into fighting organs.

The political situation that made this possible is generally referred to in the historiography of the Russian Revolution as "dyarchy" (*dvoevlastie*).[5] This expression was no mere invention of Lenin in his "Letters from Abroad." It was used already in the first days of the revolution by adherents of bourgeois Duma parties and their affiliated newspapers as a means of combatting the ambitions of the Petrograd Soviet. The Soviet majority, however, rejected this expression. The division of power between the Provisional Government and the Petrograd Soviet is quite correctly regarded as a decisive and central fact, at least in the first months of the revolution. The issue of the future revolutionary authority in Russia also produced from the very outset divergent views within the Petrograd Soviet itself.

These differences continued and were exacerbated until October.

Trotsky spoke of "the paradox of the February Revolution," referring to the voluntary renunciation by the Petrograd Soviet of the seizure of power by the revolutionary democracy, possible at the time of the fall of the monarchy. On closer examination, however, this thesis proves fictitious. Neither its real power potential nor the spiritual preparedness of the revolutionaries was such as to enable the Petrograd Soviet in February 1917 to take over the government of the country alone. Even the Bolsheviks in Petrograd were split on that question. On March 1, only a minority in the Executive Committee of the Soviet came out in favor of a Provisional Revolutionary Government by the socialist parties, incidentally in a characteristic combination foreshadowing that of October: three Bolsheviks, one Left SR, one Mezhduraionnyi,[6] two unaffiliated soldiers. The opposition — at that time standing for a coalition government with the bourgeois groups — was nearly of the same strength. As is known, the majority decided on March 2 for that conditional support of the Provisional Government combined with a simultaneous control of it by the "revolutionary soviet democracy," based on the formula *postolku-poskolku* (insofar as), which has entered the historical vocabulary as "dyarchy."

Since that time there has been no lack of explanations, justifications, and naturally also accusations. In fact, these differences of opinion began already in the first hours of the agreement which Chkheidze, Sokolov, Steklov, and Sukhanov had worked out with the Duma Committee. Within the first three weeks of March — until the arrival of Tseretelli from Irkutsk — the Soviet majority could not decide whether to stress assistance to the Provisional Government or distrustful, vigilant control. The *Izvestiaa* of the Soviet, edited by Steklov, urged the "hard" course, but this was more a hysterical reaction to alleged counterrevolutionary plots than a

---

5. Usually translated as "dual power" — Ed.

6. Trotsky's splinter Marxist group, which joined the Bolshevik party that spring — Ed.

carefully established program. The Siberian group of Mensheviks and Socialist Revolutionaries (the "Siberian Zimmerwaldists") then on its way to the capital, looked in vain for clear lines in the announcements of the Soviet organ. Considering, on the one hand, the revolutionary atmosphere, the external circumstances, and the capability of the Soviet leaders and, on the other, the urgent problems of the day, no such clear lines could have been expected.

Posterior historical analysis, however, may find some reason for the decision of the Soviet majority to assume the stance of "the controlling organ of revolutionary democracy," at some distance from the Provisional Government. The seemingly most obvious explanation is the weightiest. That handful of socialist intellectuals, whose very names were hardly familiar to the public, grew frightened of the burden of power, feeling that exercise of government demands more than a few revolutionary ideas and skillful tactics. The hour of the collapse of the monarchy and situation in the streets of the capital were anything but conducive to the seizure of power. The experiences of the Revolution of 1905 were not sufficient to produce a concrete plan of power seizure. The form of the organization itself, namely the soviet, as Trotsky correctly remarked, was "beyond discussion," but the revolutionary tradition as handed down from the Petersburg Soviet of Workers' Deputies of 1905 did not contain the political program of a government based on soviets. The almost simultaneous formation of the Duma Committee, which in spite of its own insecurity and casual composition could better claim to act as the representative of the whole state, relieved the Soviet leaders in the early stages from the responsibility of making an unequivocal decision on the question of power seizure.

In his speech at the All-Russian Conference of the Soviets of Workers' and Soldiers' Deputies on March 30, Steklov gave a precise description of the situation:

Why is it that at that moment we did not consider the question of taking power into our hands? I will attempt to answer this.... At the time when this agreement [with the Temporary Committee of the Duma] was contemplated, it was not at all clear as to whether the revolution would emerge victorious, either in a revolutionary-democratic form or even in a moderate-bourgeois form. Those of you, comrades, who were not here in Petrograd and did not experience this revolutionary fever cannot imagine how we lived: The Duma was surrounded by soldiers' platoons that did not even have any noncommissioned officers; we did not have time even to formulate any political program for the movement and at the same time we learned that the ministers were at large and were convening somewhere, either in the Admiralty, or in the Mariinskii Palace. We were not informed on the general attitude of the troops or the attitude of the Tsarskoe Selo garrison, and it was reported that they were marching on us. There were rumors that five regiments were marching from the north, that General Ivanov was leading 26 echelons; shooting resounded through the streets, and we had grounds to assume that this weak group that was surrounding the palace would be routed. We expected from minute to minute that they would arrive, and, if they did not shoot us, they would take us away. However, we sat proudly, like ancient Romans, and conferred, but there was no complete conviction whatsoever in the success of the revolution.

The ideological justification for a decision taken in response to a concrete situation was soon elaborated. But the theoretical explanation for abstaining from government and assuming the position of a controlling organ was not merely a kind of posterior rationalization of spontaneous decisions. It was actually rooted in the world of political ideas of the socialist parties before 1917. The discussions in the newspapers of the Soviet majority or in the Petrograd Soviet itself to justify the attitudes of the "revolutionary democracy" and simultaneously to counter charges of inactivity, rested, above all, on the ideological thesis of the "bourgeois" character of the Russian Revolution, which forbade the participation of socialists in bourgeois government in the interests of the forthcoming socialist revolution. Steklov called this in his speech of March 30 the "basic aspect" of the decision of the Executive Committee not to attempt to take power:

You understand that the attempt on the part of the extreme revolutionary democratic forces to take power into their own hands can have a historical basis and can rely on the support of the broad national masses only in the event that moderate liberalism becomes bankrupt while carrying its program into effect. And it stands to reason that when this moment arrives, when the liberal bourgeoisie turns out to be politically incapable of carrying out its own political program and not simply satisfying the demands of national masses, and if it meets with decisive opposition in carrying out its own program and proves to be incapable of realizing the aspirations and demands of the working masses, then at this moment we may be confronted with the question of the revolutionary democratic forces seizing power against the desires and the will of broad sections of the bourgeoisie. Such a situation did not exist at the moment, and it does not exist even now. On the contrary, we have seen that the privileged ... bourgeoisie, whose representatives constitute the majority in the Provisional Government, had come to the realization that the time was such and the forces of the revolution were such that it was necessary for them to make broad, democratic concessions.

The situation after the overthrow of the tsarist regime seemed to match exactly the prognosis Martov had made in March 1905. At that time he had spoken of a possible situation in Russia "where the struggle of the proletariat to secure and develop the revolution might coincide with the struggle to take power." For this eventuality the socialists should be prepared by

organizing the proletariat in a party standing in opposition to the bourgeois democratic state. And the best way to create such an organization is to influence the bourgeois revolution from below by the pressure of the proletariat against the democracy in power. The class which is prepared for the role of an oppositional motor force ... of the revolution will also play the role of its political master should the historical events, against its ambitions, bring it close to governmental power.

The revolutionary tactics formulated by Martov, Dan, and Martynov in 1905 preshaped the relation between the soviets and the Provisional Government during the February Revolution. The spontaneous spread of "revolutionary self-government" ... operating everywhere in the open, was thought of as a means of liquidating autocracy, but also as an instrument of the "pressure" against the bourgeois democracy that hastened the revolution toward socialism. Even the historical reminiscences of the French Revolution of 1789 and of the Commune of Paris of 1871 played their part in forming "revolutionary communes" to disorganize the governmental apparatus and to prepare the soil for a broad proletarian mass party.

If one looks for an ideological basis for the attitudes of the Soviet leaders during the first hours it might be found in the abovementioned revolutionary strategy of the Mensheviks of the spring and summer of 1905. Sukhanov, who had decisively shaped the Soviet program until the middle of March, was in the same boat with the Menshevik Internationalists led by Martov. Martov himself, although criticizing the policy of the Soviet majority from May to October, had arrived by July — in accord with his basic attitudes — to the demand that "revolutionary democracy" in the form of soviets, embodying the "political self-government of the people" and the "new revolutionary statehood," take over full political power. The "oppositional motor force" of the revolution was to become its political master.

This radical Menshevik tendency is not usually given sufficient consideration by historians of the Russian Revolution. As an organized power it remained always in the minority in the Petrograd Soviet. But its ideological influence was in the first three weeks of the February Revolution stronger than at any time later: an influence favored by the feverish revolutionary excitement of the early days, by the fear of counterrevolutionary attacks, and by the political vacuum within the socialist camp, who recognized leaders were still absent from the capital.

As the socialist party groupings in the Soviet consolidated into parliamentary factions and the ideological positions gained ground, the moderate majority tried to systematize the unsettled relations between the Soviet and the Provisional Government. This occurred particularly after the return of the Siberian group whose main representatives — Tseretelli, Dan, and Gots — together with Chkheidze and Skobelev henceforth took over the Soviet Executive Committee. The basic ideological conviction that the revolution was "bourgeois" also prevailed among the new leaders of the Soviet majority — less among the Socialist Revolutionaries, more among the Mensheviks. But this was only a general framework and a form of ideological insurance. Among Soviet leaders, practical calculations, emerging from the concrete situation in which revolutionary Russia found itself, were more influential than abstract considerations. In the case of Tseretelli particularly, the all-Russian national tasks of "revolutionary democracy" emerged early, especially as concerned the fact of war. Among the leaders of the Menshevik-Socialist-Revolutionary Soviet bloc it was Tseretelli who recognized best the necessity for "revolutionary democracy" not to confine itself to one-sided class interests but to assume responsibility for the whole nation confronted with the question of war and peace. In his "Memoirs" he speaks of the "psychological break" that he and his friends experienced in the first days of March when deciding on the question whether or not to permit passage of a train with reservists moving westward from Vladivostok to the front. "Of all practical questions which the revolution had posed us, we were least prepared for this. But we felt that the old, accustomed formulas must be supplemented with new ones, in accord with the exigencies of the revolution." The train was allowed to proceed. Thus was laid the foundation of the "revolutionary defense of the country." On March 22 this line was accepted also by the Soviet Executive Committee and ten days later by an overwhelming majority at the All-Russian Conference of Soviets. The resolution drafted by Tseretelli and adopted by a majority of 325 votes against 57 with 20 abstentions, stated:

> The revolutionary people of Russia will persist in their efforts to bring about an early conclusion of peace on the basis of the brotherhood and equality of free peoples. An official renunciation of all programs of conquest on the part of all governments is a powerful means of terminating the war on such conditions.
>
> As long as these conditions have not been met, as long as the war continues, the Russian democracy recognizes that the downfall of the army, the weakening of its resistance, its strength, and its combat potential, would be the heaviest blow to the cause of freedom and to the vital interests of the country. For the purpose of [achieving] the most energetic defense against all external attacks on revolutionary Russia, and against attempts at interference in the further successes of the revolution, the Conference of the Soviets of Workers' and Soldiers' deputies calls on the democratic forces in Russia to mobilize all the vital forces of the country in all the spheres of its national life to reinforce the front and the rear. This is an imperative demand, dictated by the present moment in the life of Russia; it is essential to the success of the great revolution.

The attitude of the soviets toward the Provisional Government also received at about this time a clearer theoretical formulation. The new stress in Tseretelli's speech at the conference of April 3 lay on "the unity of national will." "The national masses," he said, "understood the nature of the immediate task and when they advanced the democratic republic as the platform on which all the people of Russia agreed, they understood that this republic would be a bourgeois republic, but that, on the other hand, it would also be democratic, and one which, at that given moment, could unite around itself the proletariat, the peasantry, and all the groups of the bourgeoisie which understood the immediate task before the whole nation."

This policy could also be interpreted in the way Trotsky did when he wrote that at the moment of revolutionary ascendancy the moderate Soviet leaders did not feel themselves called upon "to assume leadership of the people — they preferred to form the left wing of the bourgeois order." He omitted, however, to add that this bourgeois order represented in the eyes of the leaders of the Soviet and even in those of the Bolsheviks in Russia led by Kamenev, an enormous revolutionary achievement against the tsarist regime, a decisive step forward on the way to a socialist democracy. The discussions at the All-Russian Conference of the Soviets showed surprising unanimity on the relationship between Soviets and Provisional Government. The final resolution was unanimously adopted, being supported even by the Bolsheviks.[7] It stated, among other things:

7. Lenin had not yet imposed his policies on the party — Ed.

The Conference recognizes the necessity of gradually gaining political control and influence over the Provisional Government and its local organs in order to induce it to pursue the most energetic struggle against counterrevolutionary forces, to take the most resolute steps in the direction of a complete democratization of all walks of Russian life, and to make preparations for universal peace without annexations and indemnities based on the self-determination of nations.

The Conference appeals to the democracy to lend its support to the Provisional Government without assuming responsibility for all the work of government, in so far as the Government is working steadfastly in the direction of regulating and expanding revolutionary gains and in so far as the formulation of its foreign policy is based on the renunciation of ambitions of terrotorial expansion.

Only Lenin's unconditional fight against the Provisional Government put an end to this attempt at a common policy by the "revolutionary democracy."

## Theodore H. Von Laue

# THE WEAKNESS OF GOVERNMENTAL AUTHORITY

Theodore Von Laue (1916- ), professor of history at Clark University, has written extensively on Russian history in the late nineteenth and early twentieth centuries, and has studied the impact of global political and economic forces in recent history in *The Global City: Freedom, Power and Necessity in the Age of World Revolution* (1969). In the selection below, he examines the efforts of the Provisional Government to adapt its Western concept of political authority to the crucial area of food policy.

"WESTERNIZATION" ... stands for the massive transfer of these hard visible aspects of Western civilization from England (and the United States), France, Germany, etc., into unprepared societies where the molecule of indigenous society is composed differently and where the impact is bound to fester. The history of Westernization, I think, makes clear that such a transfer has always stemmed from an unwelcome necessity rather than from preference. It is forced on the recipient for the sake of survival (although it is doubtful in the end what native tradition will survive). Everywhere Westernization has come as a subversive force undermining native authority; for native authority obviously did not endow the country with the political or cultural ascendancy which enabled it to export rather than import basic guidelines of human development. In modern Russian history we can see that Western subversion clearly at work, never more powerfully than in the half-century before 1914. It spread its nets in terms of government, society, economic well-being, expectations of the good

From Theodore Von Laue, "Westernization, Revolution and the Search for a Basis of Authority — Russia in 1917," *Soviet Studies,* XIX (October, 1967), pp. 157-170. Reprinted by permission of the editors.

life, in terms of literary taste or fashion. Against this current the tsarist regime had no recourse, try as it might. Indeed, there were powerful forces within the government pressing for more drastic modernization; Russia, they said, was rapidly falling behind in the competition with the industrialized Great Powers. If proof was needed for these alarms, the world war amply supplied it. Of all the prompters of Westernization, military defeat by a more Westernized power is the most persuasive. It compels the sacrifice of any tradition that obstructs the adoption of the Western technique of power. But what are the Western techniques of power?

The question is not easily answered, because the Western model is by no means clear-cut or precise. To start with, the Western model offers a bewildering choice, English, American, French, German, to mention but the chief sub-models at the time of the first world war, and within each of these a whole keyboard of attitudes and convictions. Yet there is worse confusion. On the one hand Westernization encourages imitation of its instruments of power, its institutions and other visible and transferable details. On the other hand it teaches that the greatest strength of a people lies within itself, in its sovereignty: the English (or the Americans) do not imitate; they are wholly themselves, both culturally and politically. This form of imitation, the deliberate assertion of native ways, sometimes encourages the most deep-seated nativism and a return to backwardness which in the end defeats itself. The same paradox occurs as the result of yet another Western import: democracy. Democracy encourages self-expression, self-determination, freedom and spontaneity. These temptations inevitably stir up the depths of tradition, sometimes to the fullness of anti-Westernism. They also affirm and harden every shade of native variety, imperilling whatever precarious unity a country had evolved in the past. Westernization thus always implies a mixture at best, an uneasy merger of native and Western elements as the imports infiltrate into the non-Western environment, and at worst a mortal conflict between incompatible sources of basic inspiration (or authority). What we find then in any society under Western influence is a wide spectrum of inchoate combinations, ambiguity, contradiction, indecision, and a wrangle of many souls in one breast. Thus Westernization enters as a divisive force into a society already burdened with discord.

And finally, Westernization cannot but draw state and society into closer ties with the advanced Western model. This implies more strenuous interaction in terms of economic relations and power politics in peace and war. Whatever form such interaction takes — and it is most arduous in times of war — it will put the country under a tighter necessity of efficiency. It will impose a higher degree of specialization, extort a harder and seemingly more self-denying work discipline, compel a more subtle rationality among individuals and institutions and demand more cohesion and common purpose in society at large just when they are more than ever lacking as a result of Westernization. Such are the unsettling effects of Westernization, and Russia in the throes of revolution showed all of them (though only a few can be pointed out here).

The February revolution itself might be interpreted as the product of Westernization. It embodied the political ideals of constitutional government and democracy as practised in the West and the heightened expectations derived from the prewar contacts with Western Europe; it was fed from the tensions built up by the rapid Westernization and industrialization since the 1890s. It also reflected the wartime pressure for still more rapid modernization, particularly of the army and the economy. The tsarist regime had patently failed to protect the country. It was the task of its successor to introduce a superior efficiency, first in the political framework of the country, and then in everything else that mattered for the national welfare in war and peace.

Let the term revolution be applied, however, more specifically to the eight months between the collapse of the tsarist regime and the Bolshevik coup, when even Lenin would boast that Russia was the freest country in the world. Let it also stand for the lengthy revolutionary chain reaction set off by the February revolution. Since March the people of Russia possessed the freedom to agitate and organize, to express at last their deepest thoughts and feelings, without fear of consequences. In both its dual centres the new government left no doubt that it welcomed such self-expression. As the Provisional Government announced on 7 March, while defending the country "the Government will at the same time deem it to be its primary duty to open a way to the expression of the popular will with regard to the form of government ... and ... to provide the country with laws safeguarding civil liberty and equality in order to enable all citizens to apply freely their spiritual forces to creative work for the benefit of the country". The Petrograd Soviet trumpeted a more drastic version of the same message to its following: "We must take the fullest advantage of the present state of affairs. Everyone must form associations, a free press must be created, and meetings must be called where the freedom of speech must be exercised in a tireless struggle against the old order.... Form associations, call meetings — agitate! Remember that every minute is valuable during a revolution.... The chief strength of the democracy lies in its organization!" The order of the day was: agitate, activate, organize, and agitate again with redoubled strength and make your influence felt to the limits of your organization. And the inhabitants of the empire did organize after March as they had never before.

Propertied and educated Russia was well organized already. Its agencies were ready, the Fourth Duma supplemented by members of its predecessors, the State Council[1] still hovering in the background, the many organizations of trade and industry, and, of course, the party organization of the Kadets now enlarged and strengthened. Among those who had hitherto been deprived of the opportunity, new organizations sprang up like mushrooms; the soviets were only the chief among innumerable lesser groups. It was inevitable that this process of articulating public opinion under the Western slogan of democratic freedom should stir up layers of the population that had traditionally stood entirely outside politics. This process, called "the deepening of the revolution", must be judged the single most crucial corollary of the revolution of freedom. It was bound to mobilize the furthest recesses of Russian tradition and throw all varieties of outlook and interest and levels of civilization within the empire into stark surface relief.

Let it be pointed out next that in this frenzy of agitation and organization all competitors started with equal opportunities. The race was wide open to what was called "all the live creative forces of the country". Only time would reveal where the handicaps lay. At the outset at least the "censitary" elements[2] patently possessed the strongest assets in their social position and their widely acknowledged experience of public affairs. Yet once under way the process was entirely a matter of trial and error, an exploration of the hidden opportunities of mass politics in the Russian setting. No one could foresee at the time whither it would lead.

Thus the peoples of Russia, with unprecedented suddenness, were propelled into the age of mass politics and thrust up, unprepared, against the problem of reconstituting their government by voluntary agreement. It was a staggering challenge: how in all the seething agitation through the length and breadth of the country could there emerge a central authority sufficient for preserving law and order, preventing a collapse of the economy, and carrying the war to a solution reasonably in line with national interest? The progress of the revolution between February and October added up to an elemental search for a basis of "a stable, resolute and single revolutionary authority" as an alternative to chaos and the

---

1. The State Council was the largely appointive upper body of the Russian legislature between 1905 and 1917 — Ed.

2. Those Russians who had enjoyed the right to vote in tsarist times — Ed.

annihilation of Russia's sovereignty. It is important to note, however, that all spokesmen, from the Kadet right to the Bolshevik left, accepted the basic premise that such authority was to express the will of the people, or at least their majority. Yet how this could be done or whether it was possible at all, remained to be seen. Here lay the crux of the political experiment set off by the February revolution.

Pointing to the repeated and mounting demands for a firm and stable authority is not to deny the existence of a strong counter-strain of anarchy. The sudden grant of full freedom encouraged among all layers of the population a penchant for unilateral and precipitous action not cleared with the Provisional Government. The months between February and October abounded with such licence; the unresolved dualism at the centre set a bad example. The same political leaders who called for a firm authority, furthermore, often took the lead in provoking disorders. Wherever one looks in Russia in these months, authority and anarchy were closely intertwined, and any effort to create or assert authority often aggravated the anarchy. The anarchy in turn intensified the search for authority and forced authority to become more authoritarian.

The search for a convincing authority pervaded all aspects of Russian life and government in the months after the February revolution. For a brief illustration of the consequences of that revolution this essay now turns to two vital tasks of the government: providing food and stabilizing the economy.

The supply of food to the army and to the population in the food-importing parts of Russia had posed a grave problem already before the revolution; it had led, in 1915, to the creation of a special Council on Food Supply attached to the Ministry of Agriculture. After the revolution this body was reorganized as the State Committee on Food Supplies; in early April, under strong pressure from the Soviet, it was finally transformed into a fully-fledged state grain monopoly, advised by a central State Food Committee, on which sat — under the new principle of parity representation — the spokesmen of the major forces in public opinion. As a further step toward effective administration, on 19 May a special Ministry of Food Supplies was created. In order to facilitate the work of these agencies the Provisional Government encouraged the establishment of a network of local groups, called the food committees, in the provinces, districts and towns. Eventually much of the work of the grain monopoly devolved upon these bodies: taking charge of local reserves, conducting a census of the crop lands in cultivation and supervising distribution and transportation of the grain under prices fixed by the central government. As it emerged after March, the basic pattern seemed rational enough — on paper.

In reality there was growing chaos. In the first place, one has to remember that the food monopoly was foisted on the Provisional Government by the Soviet. The business community, particularly that group which in the past had conducted the grain trade, was strongly opposed. It wanted more, not less, freedom from the revolution. Barely rid of tsarist meddling, it took the grain monopoly as an entering wedge of an ever more constringent socialism. Its opposition soon came to a head in the State Food Committee, which thus turned into a political forum. Considering the variety of groups represented on it and the widening divergence of their views, it was not surprising that this body, which was to rally public opinion to the support of the grain monopoly, became instead a mere debating society.

The local food committees were even less effective. They were created in only half the provinces (mostly the food-consuming ones), where they rarely acted according to official instructions. The food-producing provinces, on the other hand, proved for the most part extremely uncooperative, even to the point of sabotaging the government's efforts. Where local food committees were established, they became involved in all the tensions of their community and changed their political complexion as opinions became more inflamed. By the autumn they were often taking the law into their own hands, after breaking all ties with the capital. It was no wonder then that as early as May the Provisional Government tried to shift their function to the zemstvos,[3] hoping thereby to introduce greater orderliness. But the zemstvos, too, were caught in the turmoil and incapable of shouldering additional burdens. And as if it had no confidence in its local organs, already in April the government had begun to dispatch special emissaries into the countryside. As S. N. Prokopovich admitted in May: "We have to extract the grain from the people with the assistance of special expeditions."

In Western Europe — to put the matter into perspective — the problem of gathering and distributing food for the purposes of war was comparatively easy. The state made use of existing commercial channels for the grain trade, endowing them with the necessary additional controls. In Russia, however, it quickly became apparent that the services of private business were not wanted. The local food committees and other public elements associated with them, like the soviets, were particularly hostile to any participation by commercial agents; the grain merchants were among the most hated of all "capitalists". Here and there, to be sure, their cooperation was solicited; but most committees would have nothing to do with them, even to the detriment of their duties. There were cases where local committees were dissolved under local pressure, just because they had relied on "capitalists." A.V. Peshekhonov, the Minister of Food, conceded in June that sometimes these merchants had earned this hostility by speculation and dishonesty so that even the tsarist government had begun to bypass them.

Needless to say, the deep-seated hostility between large elements of the population and the grain traders undermined the grain monopoly. By October it was about to collapse. Its abolition was openly discussed in the Ministry of Trade and Industry, which wanted to substitute a bureaucratic apparatus working through commercial channels. This new approach (never carried out) was a part of the hardening of the liberal attitude in the last months before the Bolshevik seizure of power. Another indication of the failure of the grain monopoly was a doubling of the fixed prices of food in September, which could only benefit the producers, particularly the large ones, at the expense of the small consumers. In the absence of a more effective authority, the step may have been necessary in order to bring the hidden reserves to market, but it undermined the public confidence in the grain monopoly. The peasants, too, hastened its débâcle by evading the crop census ordered by the government, by forcibly preventing the transport of grain, or by illegally distilling it and thereby contributing to the drunken orgies that sometimes accompanied rural disorders. The grain monopoly thus ran up against the innate localism, the anti-capitalism and the plain anarchy of peasant life.

It was not, however, all stubbornness and ignorance that made the peasant and other producers so anarchic. As long as they received ever less in return for their labours they could not be expected to part with their stores. This realization had prompted the Minister of Agriculture at the very start of the grain monopoly to set up a section in his ministry aiming to provide the peasants with cheap consumer goods, as well as with machinery and fertilizers. This task was taken over in May by the new Ministry of Food Supplies; it became in effect the Ministry of Supplies and Consumer Goods in general (not without competition from the Ministry of Trade and Industry, a far more "capitalist" ministry, which soon created its own supply committee). The ambition to supply Russia with all necessities, however, had vast implications; it called for no less than state control of the entire economy, of production, distribution, consumption and transportation.

It should be remembered in this context that the chief problem facing the Provisional Government in the administration of the grain monopoly was not an overall shortage

---

3. Local representative assemblies inherited from the tsarist regime — Ed.

of grain. Sufficient reserves were left over from the 1916 harvest; and the next harvest was by no means as disastrous as one might deduce from the drift of politics in the summer and autumn of 1917. The problem was primarily one of organizing the collection and distribution of existing stores. That, however, called for a firm and stable authority capable not only of overcoming the conflicting social and political pressures at work among the local and central agencies of the grain monopoly, but also of finding a speedy solution to the land problem, as well as of salvaging Russia's collapsing economy.

Turning now to the economy as a whole, one might well argue that, given the weakness of the transportation systems and the strains of the war, nothing could have stopped the galloping breakdown. The more the railways were worn out by the over-use of equipment, the more trade and industry were bound to suffer; the more their activities were curtailed, the less fuel and metal would reach the railways — in an ever narrowing spiral leading to a dead end. This, however, was not the prognosis of the leading public figures in any camp; they were full of hope. Unfortunately they could not agree over the proper remedies; and their wrangle over economic policy revealed yet another facet of the search for a strong authority.

For the guidance of the economy the Provisional Government had inherited the machinery of economic mobilization devised in 1915 by the Progressive Bloc[4] and its allies among the public and the bureaucracy. Essentially it consisted of the four Special Councils (for defence, fuel, transport and food — the latter already mentioned), and in addition the Central War Industries Committee, altogether a rather uncoordinated and somewhat ineffectual set of agencies. The reason for the confusion and overlapping of competence lay in the fact that the Progressive Bloc had thought the tsarist bureaucracy incapable of achieving the fullest mobilization of Russian industry. The question after March 1917 was whether the new government could impose more effective and better coordinated controls.

The Provisional Government started on its difficult task with the basic assumption that more public participation in the controlling agencies, both central and local, would liberate the creative energies of the Russian people. Thus the bureaucrats on the afore-mentioned councils were largely replaced by delegates from public bodies, from the soviets, the various organizations of trade, industry and finance, the cooperatives (whose role was rapidly increasing), the trade unions, the peasant soviets and similar organizations. At the same time the Provisional Government tried to liberate private initiative through the enactment, immediately after the revolution, of a new corporation law, which gave rise to a minor speculative boom. From March to the summer an unusually large number of new enterprises were incorporated — in the eyes of Russian businessmen the long-awaited opportunity had at last come. Now they hoped to acquire the prosperity and social prestige appropriate to their position in the capitalist era. There was nothing reactionary in their outlook. Following the Western model, they were for the most part ready to support a progressive labour policy, provided, of course, that the rights of management went unchallenged.

Whether this programme could have reversed the drift towards collapse depended on the loyal compliance of the working class. Yet the Russian workers were hardly in the mood to accept the authority of the capitalists, for they too expected to make the most of their new freedom. The February revolution introduced democracy into the very heart of private enterprise. In one of its first measures the Provisional Government, under the pressure of the Soviet, had legalized the factory committees, elected bodies of workers all too ready to encroach on the rights of management. These factory committees sprang up with great speed, more rapidly than the more elaborate trade unions, and were patently more expressive

---

4. Duma coalition formed in 1915 under the leadership of the Cadets — Ed.

of the mentality of the workers. They instinctively tended to tighten the cohesion of the work force, sometimes by throwing out men of non-working class (or non-peasant) background. They were also likely to view the factory as the peasants viewed the land, as a source of livelihood that rightly belonged to them. When the management threatened to shut down production, for lack of fuel, raw materials, operating funds, or of plain entrepreneurial energy in exceedingly difficult times, the factory committees often attempted to run the factories themselves. Under these conditions the relations between the *fabkomy*[5] and the management were strained at best, and production inevitably suffered. This was obviously no time to impose tight labour discipline. The incessant political activities of hitherto passive workers, the uncertainties of the time, the falling purchasing power of their wages, the material difficulties of life in general, which always hit the workers hardest — all contributed to the growing anarchy in the factories, mills and mines. Was it a wonder that in their new freedom the workers were speaking their own minds, untutored though they were in the rationalities of industry and commerce or in the complexities of modern society, and if they spoke with a vengeance?

In May the crisis in industrial relations exploded into the government through the resignation of the Minister of Trade and Industry, A. I. Konovalov, one of the most enlightened spokesmen of the Russian business community. In a speech shortly before his resignation he issued a sharp warning: "The slogans which are being thrust into the midst of the workers, exciting the dark instincts of the mob, are followed by destruction, anarchy, and the annihilation of public and national life." In other words, democracy as the workers saw it was incompatible with industrial production sufficient to carry on the war and to supply the population with the necessities of life.

Yet there was another threat that drove Konovalov to despair: undue pressure on the Provisional Government from the Soviet and from its representative in the cabinet, the Minister of Labour, M. I. Skobelev. For under Menshevik inspiration the Soviet, too, had analysed the economic crisis and drawn up its own recommendations (formulated by V. G. Groman).

The Soviet leadership viewed the economic goals of the revolution very differently from the business community. It felt no scruples over the extension of government control. Groman admired the British and still more the German system of wartime industrial mobilization; as a Marxist he rejoiced in phrases like "the planned regulation of economic life." In May the Soviet stepped forward with plans for 1) the compulsory cartellization of the industries concerned with coal, oil, metals, sugar, paper; 2) governmental control of all banks and credit institutions; and 3) universal labour conscription after the German model "in order to combat idleness". Finally, it demanded greatly stepped-up taxation of income and profits. Even Lenin found these plans somewhat extreme; they were unacceptable, of course, to the Provisional Government. Prokopovich, eventually Konovalov's successor, argued that, while such things were possible in England or Germany, Russia was not ready for them.

Under Soviet pressure, however, the Provisional Government ordered the four ministries most directly concerned (Trade and Industry, Finance, Labour and Food Supply) to draft a proposal for an effective economic policy. One of the results was a memorandum written by V. A. Stepanov, the acting minister of trade and industry. It was a curious document containing two contradictory recommendations. On the one hand, it said that the Provisional Government must make it clear once and for all that Russia was heading for a "capitalist order". On the other hand he admitted that "the government cannot recommend to the country a return to a free economy.... The economic disorder does not allow a predominance of private interests." He went so

---

5. Russian abbreviation for "factory committee" — Ed.

far as to advocate the imitation of the German model of compulsory cartellization for whole branches of industry, and government regulation of labour relations as well.

This memorandum revealed the confusion created by dual power in the field of economic policy. Neither a clear-cut principle of action nor a forthright authority arose to guide the economic development in times of disintegration. Was it surprising then that the government favoured a debilitating compromise? In June it created an Economic Council charged with drafting "a general plan for the organization of the national economy and of labour" and a subsidiary Central Economic Committee charged with carrying out its recommendations. At the same time it packed these bodies with a majority of "capitalists" under the leadership of leading industrialists.

The Economic Council was a large body containing, besides the representatives of the ministries concerned, the delegates of the Soviet, the Congresses of Trade and Industry, of the banks, cooperatives, the grain traders, trade unions, zemstvos and professional economists. With such diversity of outlook the Economic Council shared the fate of the State Food Committee and quickly degenerated into a debating society. In September it was dissolved, under the pressure of the business community, having accomplished nothing. Its functions were absorbed by the Central Economic Committee, which had less ambitious talks and did not raise ideological questions. The suppression of the Economic Council, incidentally, was yet another step in the efforts of the propertied elements to consolidate their position in the interval between the failure of Kornilov and the Bolshevik coup.

The currency and the budget, too, faced chaos in those months. It came as a shock when N. V. Nekrasov, the Minister of Finance, announced at the Moscow State Conference that the revolution had been far more extravagant financially than the autocracy. This was not entirely surprising, considering that the revolt against the tsarist regime had been, in some respects, also a revolt against poverty. Now that the former penny-pinching authority had been overthrown, the many new public authorities that succeeded it spent more freely and irresponsibly. But something more ominous was involved. A zemstvo official reported on the same occasion that he had found a strange attitude in the countryside: money was a bourgeois institution and therefore could be spent to one's heart's content. "Never", so he reported, "had there been such reckless spending." Thus state expenditures skyrocketed while tax receipts fell off sharply, compelling the government to resort ever more freely to the printing press for its supply of money.

Taxation was another political issue undermining the authority of the Provisional Government. The tsarist government had introduced the income tax in 1916; in May and June of 1917, under pressure from the Soviet, its successor sharply increased the income tax as well as the tax on war profits, though not as radically as the Soviet had desired. Before the Bolshevik coup the high rates, however, were reduced again in view of the financial distress of the propertied classes (this again was part of the hardening of the liberal attitude). The Liberty Loan proclaimed soon after the February revolution, was a further effort on the part of the new government to tap the financial reserves of the country and to limit the rampant inflation. Yet it did not catch hold. The working classes could not and would not save, and the "capitalists" in their apprehension held back. By autumn the loan was considered a relative failure. The slow returns on the loan prompted plans for a more drastic capital levy, which, however, were not carried out either. The "egotism" of the propertied classes did not go unobserved and uncriticized, even among moderates. Yet in the absence of a firm and stable authority one can hardly blame the "capitalists" for taking what private precautions they could: their worst traits were reinforced by the general insecurity. This meant widespread speculation, black-market operations and sometimes irresponsibly high living.

The economic decline accentuated the traditional sharp inequalities in Russian society. The government and every important political leader, including Lenin, constantly urged the utmost sacrifices for the cause of the country. But it remained an open question who was making such sacrifices and who was to judge how real and extensive they were. From May onwards, each group was accusing the others of "narrow class feeling", but in the end the opinion of the largest number, i.e. of the workers, soldiers and peasants, carried the day. The deep-seated egalitarianism of the peasant *soslovie* ["estate"—Ed.] was running stronger than ever, now that it could be openly expressed. Anybody living in a better style, so peasant opinion argued, should be making a proportionately greater sacrifice until he had reached the common level; and who could deny that from the material point of view the toilers were still worse off than the *burzhui*? In these months of rapidly deteriorating conditions hunger and cold thus divided the Russian polity ever more deeply and broke down whatever authority and prestige had accrued to the privileged classes during the good years before the war. Hunger and cold also aggravated the divisions over basic economic policy.

One may describe the opposing positions in the economic struggle roughly as follows. On the one hand we find the supporters of a system of free enterprise modified, as in England, by progressive labour legislation and by the necessities of the war cautiously interpreted. They wanted to leave the right of management untouched; workers' control was anathema to them, as was central control by a state planning agency. They knew from experience that the workers were not qualified to run the factories according to the demands of modern competition efficiency (within the country as well as in the international market); and they agreed with Prokopovich that under Russian conditions effective planning, even of the kind at work in wartime Germany, was hopelessly utopian. Finally, they argued that after the war Russia would need large foreign loans; these could be obtained only from Western capitalists for capitalist purposes.

Their opponents, on the other hand, marshalled an equally strong rebuttal. Given the conditions of Russia, it was obvious that all aspects of the economy were interdependent. If there was to be enough food, manufactured goods had to reach the village; they had to be produced in sufficient quantities, under priorities determined by the needs of state and society. Given the scarcities, furthermore, consumption too would have to be regulated. Under the hard necessities of the moment, therefore, the socialist economists might seem to have had the best of the argument. Only a central and all-encompassing authority could undertake the rational revival of the economy. The socialist view, however, was deficient in regard to the details of planning: how were the central plans to be carried out at the grass-roots? Thus again the question of authority was raised. The Menshevik planners assumed, of course, that with the widest possible democratic participation the problem could be solved. But that assumption the "capitalists", with a more realistic experience of the working class, knew to be false.

The conflict of rival interests and panaceas dissolved whatever central authority over the Russian economy the Provisional Government had inherited. Eventually production and distribution became a matter of catch-as-catch-can. Even before the Bolshevik coup Petrograd was informed that in certain areas of the country the economy was lapsing into a state of barter. Manufactured goods of local production were being exchanged against local foodstuffs. Only a strong central authority with strong local agents and an effective administrative apparatus could restore an effective national economy.

*Harvey Asher*

# THE DEFEAT OF MILITARY LEADERSHIP

One of the decisive moments in the political evolution of the Russian Revolution was the conflict between General Kornilov, the most powerful figure in the Russian Army, and the Provisional Government. Why did the revolt occur and what were the two sides seeking to accomplish? Harvey Asher, professor of history at Drury College, Springfield, Missouri, looks at the events which led up to the clash to determine the real motives of the participants and finds that both leaders sought at the outset to strengthen the regime against the extremists.

ONLY SIX months after the relatively peaceful February Revolution that ended tsarist rule, Russia appeared on the verge of civil war. On September 9,[1] Alexander Kerensky, head of the Provisional Government, appealed to the people to resist an alleged attempt of the Commander-in-Chief of the Army, General L. G. Kornilov, to overthrow the government. The majority of the population rallied to the support of the Provisional Government and the Soviets, thereby dooming Kornilov's enterprise to failure. On September 14 the General surrendered and the supposed rebellion was over.

In the confusion of the time, few questioned the accuracy of the government's contention or its right to defend itself and the revolution from reactionary elements. After the crisis had passed and the passions of the moment had given way to more sober reflection, it became obvious to many that the official government version of the episode was not entirely satisfactory. Since 1917 a prodigious amount of literature has appeared, seeking to establish exactly what happened during these five crucial days in the history of the Russian revolution. Major Western scholarship on the subject includes the representative and conflicting arguments of Abraham Ascher and Leonid Strakhovsky.[2]

Ascher is highly critical of Kornilov's role, much less so of that of Kerensky. Ascher has no doubt that Kornilov rebelled against the Provisional Government, intending to use as a pretext for his own action a Bolshevik uprising supposedly scheduled for September 10-11 on the half-year anniversary of the revolution.... He admits that, at one point, Kerensky may have inadvertently encouraged Kornilov to believe that the General had the government's sanction for his planned purge of disruptive elements in Petrograd but that later Kerensky learned that he as well as the Bolsheviks and other radicals were to be removed by Kornilov.... Hence Kerensky acted properly in dismissing Kornilov and in using force when Kornilov refused to relinquish his post.

Strakhovsky challenged this interpretation, arguing that the real villain of the episode was Kerensky, who by deliberately betraying Kornilov delivered Russia into the hands of the Bolsheviks.... Kornilov was the only man who could have infused

---

1. Dates in this article follow the New Style, Western calendar – Ed.

2. Abraham Ascher, "The Kornilov Affair," *Russian Review*, XII (October, 1953), 235-252; Leonid Strakhovsky, "Was There a Kornilov Rebellion — A Reappraisal of the Evidence," *Slavonic and East European Review*, XXXIII (June, 1955), 372-395.

From Harvey Asher, "The Kornilov Affair: A Reinterpretation," *Russian Review*, XXIX (January, 1970), 286-300. Reprinted by permission of the editors.

strength into a government which found itself increasingly a prisoner of the Petrograd Soviet. According to Strakhovsky, Kornilov was not a counterrevolutionary and never planned a revolt against the Provisional Government, but believed that he was working with it to suppress the Bolsheviks and other radicals. His abrupt dismissal by Kerensky came as a shock, and he could only assume that Kerensky had fallen completely under the influence of the Soviet. When Kornilov refused to surrender his command, it was obviously an act of insubordination, "but certainly not of mutiny or rebellion as Kerensky wanted it to appear".... The disparities in these two articles and the tendentious and polemical nature of the literature as a whole suggest the purpose of this essay — to offer a new and fairer interpretation of the Kornilov Affair.

It is not necessary to recount in great detail Kornilov's biography.... Yet several incidents indicative of Kornilov's outlook and suggestive of his future relationship with Kerensky are worth mentioning. In April 1915, while Russia's armies were being driven from Galicia, Kornilov was captured by the enemy. His dramatic escape from an Austro-Hungarian prison camp made his name favorably known throughout Russia and provided a welcome contrast to the usual dismal reports of military actions. During the first days of the February Revolution, Kornilov was named commander of the military district of Petrograd. He resigned this post during the April demonstrations against the policy of Foreign Minister Miliukov when it became apparent that Kornilov could not impose his will on the Soviet. Here began the antagonism between Kornilov and the Soviet which was to harden in the future.

On May 8, Kornilov became commander of the Eighth Army on the southwestern front. During the unsuccessful July offensive,[3] when his own army was one of the few to distinguish itself, he sent a telegram to the Provisional Government urging reestablishment of the death penalty and of court-martials in theaters of military operation. The proposal is important, for it marks the beginning of the disagreement between Kornilov and Kerensky over when and how to restore military discipline. When the government refused to implement Kornilov's plan immediately, he acted vigorously in his own area. On July 21, Kornilov ordered all commanders subordinate to him to turn machine guns and artillery on units which abandoned their positions without permission. In this manner, Kornilov established a reputation as a stern disciplinarian, who, when necessary, was willing to act independently.

Kornilov's image as a "strong man" was further enhanced as a result of a conference held at Stavka[4] on July 29, in the wake of the July defeats. Kerensky, recently named Prime Minister of the Provisional Government, and all the generals, especially Denikin, blamed the failure of the recent offensive on the soldiers' demoralization, induced by Order #1 and other legislation which sought to democratize the army. Kornilov did not attend, but his views, sent by telegram, were more conciliatory. He proposed to restore the death penalty and military revolutionary tribunals within the theater of military operations and to limit, but not abolish, the authority of soldiers' committees in economic and routine matters. He wished to prohibit meetings and antipatriotic propaganda at the front. On the role of political commissars with the army, he even proposed that this institution be reinforced. Finally, Kornilov demanded a purification of the High Command, implying that the disaster was not solely the fault of the soldiers. Kerensky said, "Such a view tended to produce the impression that here was a man with a deeper and wider outlook upon the situation than that of his compeers." Consequently, on August 1 he ap-

---

3. The July (June) Offensive involved a major attack on the Austro-Hungarian army, which quickly turned into a serious defeat for the Russian troops — Ed.

4. General headquarters of the Russian army, in the city of Mogilev — Ed.

pointed Kornilov to be Supreme Commander-in-Chief.

The circumstances of the appointment were far from pleasant. Kornilov listed four conditions the government had to accept before he would agree to assume command: (1) his responsibility would be to his own conscience and to the whole people; (2) the government would not interfere in his operative orders and in the appointment of the higher commanding staff; (3) use of the death penalty would be extended to the rear where any reinforcements were stationed; (4) the government would endorse proposals he had submitted on July 29. Kerensky was especially disturbed by the first point, which, if literally interpreted, gave Kornilov unlimited powers. He seriously considered dismissing Kornilov, but the majority of the members of the Provisional Government did not agree.

On August 2, meanwhile, Kornilov refused to approve Kerensky's appointment of General V. A. Cheremisov as commander-in-chief of the southwestern front. Kornilov disapproved of Cheremisov's sympathy for the Soviet and argued that the appointment violated his right to select the command staff. Kerensky retreated, and Kornilov's candidate, P.S. Baluev, replaced Cheremisov. In return for this concession, Kornilov accepted an interpretation by Filonenko, the political commissar at Stavka, that responsibility to the people also meant responsibility to the Provisional Government. It was only on August 6, five days after his appointment, that Kornilov assumed his new duties at Mogilev.

The reconciliation of Kornilov and Kerensky over the former's appointment was largely one of appearance, as fundamental differences between the two remained. Boris Savinkov, the man who had been influential in securing Kornilov's appointment, now took it upon himself to get the Prime Minister and the Supreme Commander to cooperate. Savinkov had been appointed Deputy Minister of War on August 6, and he soon became Kerensky's right-hand man in military matters. Yet he himself had marked disagreements with Kerensky, especially because the latter, almost daily, spoke of removing Kornilov from his command and of assuming the post himself. Savinkov first met Kornilov when Savinkov was commander of the southwestern front and was impressed not only by the General's military prowess, but by the more important fact that here was a leader whose men obeyed him. After reassuring himself that Kornilov had no intention of setting himself up as a dictator, Savinkov brought him to the attention of Kerensky, who shortly thereafter appointed him Supreme Commander-in-Chief.

At Savinkov's suggestion, Kornilov visited Kerensky in the capital on August 16. He brought with him a four-point program for the restoration of army discipline, approved beforehand by Savinkov, which called for military revolutionary tribunals in the rear as well as at the front and called for the abrogation of Order #1. At the meeting, Kerensky rebuked Kornilov for making his reports to the government sound like ultimatums. Kornilov replied that his demands were not prompted by personal feelings but by the needs of the situation. When Kerensky asked Kornilov's opinion about his own remaining in office, the General replied that Kerensky's influence had weakened but he should remain at his post. A second incident occurred which further strained relations between the two men. While Kornilov was addressing the cabinet on where the Russian armies might launch future offensive operations, he was interrupted by Kerensky, who passed him a note suggesting that he not speak so freely before the Council of Ministers because not all of its members were trustworthy. (The reference was to Chernov, the Social Revolutionary Minister of Agriculture.) This only confirmed Kornilov's notion of the weakness and insecurity of the government....

Thus as the Moscow State Conference opened on August 25, Kornilov and Kerensky appeared to be moving farther apart. Kerensky correctly surmised that if he implemented Kornilov's program — especially the proposal to reestablish the death penalty in the rear — it would mean a break with the

Petrograd Soviet, a move that he was not yet prepared to make. He still had hopes that at the Moscow State Conference he could attract mass support and thereby strengthen his position vis à vis Kornilov. In turn, the General, irritated by Kerensky's stalling tactics regarding his program, now sought to recruit allies in case he had to push his program without the support of the Provisional Government.

The purpose of the Conference was to aid the Provisional Government to find a source of mass support for itself among the progressive forces of Russia. More than 2400 delegates attended, presumably divided equally between the Right and the Left. With the opening of the Conference came a general strike organized by the Bolsheviks, who did not participate in the Conference. Kerensky inaugurated the proceedings with a vague speech in which he tried to hide the weakness of the government by strong gestures and by warning both the Left and the Right against armed uprisings. When Kornilov arrived on August 26, he received a thunderous reception from the delegates of the Right. That evening a spokesman from the Provisional Government told the General that he would speak at the August 27 session but that he should restrict himself to questions relating to strategy on the front. In his speech, for the most part apolitical, Kornilov expressed doubt about the army's ability to perform its duty, criticized the soldiers' committees and the political commissars, and described in depressing terms the military productivity of Russian munition enterprises. He ended ominously: "It cannot be tolerated that order in the rear should come about as the result of the loss of Riga and that order on the railways should be restored by the cession of Moldavia and Bessarabia to the enemy,"[5] a statement which Soviet writers have often drawn out of context to show that Kornilov deliberately yielded these areas to the Germans.

The Moscow State Conference showed that Russia was divided into two camps, between whom agreement could not be reached. Kerensky's nervous exhaustion and loss of self-control was so great that he had to be applauded into stopping his rambling concluding speech. When he absentmindedly started to walk off the stage, he had to be recalled to bring the conference to a formal conclusion.

Disillusioned at this new failure, Kerensky informed Savinkov on August 30 that he was ready to accept Kornilov's report of August 16 in principle. On September 1, he asked Savinkov to go to headquarters to coordinate agreement between Kornilov and the government. Thus from August 30, regardless of what Kerensky said or thought afterward, he led Kornilov to believe that the General's plan could be implemented with the support of the Provisional Government. And until Kornilov received the telegram on September 9 calling for his dismissal, nothing occurred to alter this impression.

The reconciliation of Kornilov and Kerensky was further solidified between September 5-6, when Savinkov arrived at Stavka to complete the arrangements accepted by Kerensky on August 30. The Provisional Government as a whole was unaware of the negotiations, for it was not informed of Savinkov's visit until the crisis broke on September 8. After considerable argument, Savinkov and Kornilov drew up a program, the last two points of which are most significant. Kornilov agreed that the city of Petrograd proper, as against the Petrograd military district, should be exempt from subordination to the Supreme Commander-in-Chief, an indication that Kerensky still did not trust Kornilov. More important, Kornilov was asked to send the Third Corps to enforce martial law in Petrograd. Although Kerensky contends that it had not been definitely decided for what purpose the troops would be used, it is certain that Kornilov understood they would be used against the Bolsheviks and, if need be, the other parties of the Soviet if they joined Lenin's ranks. Surely Kerensky must have had the same intention; it is difficult to believe that troops dispatched by and pre-

---

5. Both areas had just fallen to the armies of the Central Powers — Ed.

sumably loyal to Kornilov could be used to act against a threatened coup by the Right. The Third Corps was presumably being called to Petrograd because Kerensky feared that publication of Kornilov's program, calling for the imposition of the death penalty in the rear, would lead to complications, namely an uprising of the Bolsheviks. In order that the Provisional Government know exactly what to do and when to publish the new law, Savinkov asked Kornilov to telegraph him when the corps was in position. The government did not wish to provoke prematurely an uprising with which it lacked the forces to cope.

By September 8, then, Kornilov's program was about to be adopted. That evening, back in Petrograd, Savinkov went to a session of the Provisional Government at which he expected final approval to be given. Instead, "Kerensky called me from the Malakhitov Hall and showed me Lvov's ultimatum." It is to this new and unexpected factor that we now turn.

V.N. Lvov, former procurator of the Holy Synod, ... was a self-appointed middleman who believed that Kornilov and Kerensky should work together. On September 4 he met with Kerensky and tried to convince him that he had no support anywhere and that the groups Lvov represented wished Kerensky to reorganize the government to include the Right kadets and certain socialists who did not belong to the Soviet. Kerensky did not give Lvov a definite answer to his proposal but encouraged him to probe further; in this way, Kerensky apparently hoped to find out the details of the counter-revolutionary plot for which he had been searching since the Moscow State Conference.

Lvov then proceeded to Stavka, where he saw Kornilov on September 7. Lvov told the General that the Prime Minister was ready to resign if Kornilov thought it necessary, but the succession of power must be legal. In view of the present situation, Kornilov himself might be chosen dictator. The General replied that he would do his duty. Kornilov also thought it desirable that Savinkov and Kerensky participate in the new administration, the former as Minister of War, the latter as Minister of Justice. Kornilov urged that because of the anticipated Bolshevik uprising of September 10, Kerensky and Savinkov should come to Stravka, for otherwise he could not be responsible for their lives. Kornilov also pledged the army's support to Kerensky.

What can we conclude? It appears that Kornilov believed Lvov spoke for Kerensky, although Lvov neither offered nor was asked for proof of his status. While uncertain of Kerensky's position, Kornilov probably decided that at a minimum the Prime Minister was willing to rearrange the government to form a strong central power. Thus, even if Kornilov had been planning a coup, a question we still have to consider, he was now convinced that Kerensky was ready to cooperate and that conspiratorial methods were no longer necessary.

But according to Kerensky, whose account both Ascher and Strakhovsky accept, when Lvov returned to see him on September 8, Lvov delivered an ultimatum in Kornilov's name which called for the establishment of martial law in Petrograd, the resignation of Kerensky and his cabinet, and the transfer of all military and civil authority into the hands of the Supreme Commander. Yet Kerensky admits that Lvov used the word "propose" rather than 'demand" in transmitting Kornilov's message. Kerensky was now convinced that Lvov's conduct was part of a larger conspiracy. "I couldn't prove it point for point, but I recognized everything with striking clarity." Clearly agitated, Kerensky suggested, and Lvov agreed, that they meet at 8 P.M. at the house of the War Minister to get direct confirmation from Kornilov over the telegraph that Lvov had correctly transmitted his proposal. At the appointed time, Lvov failed to appear. Kerensky, after holding Kornilov on the line for twenty-five minutes, decided to go through with the conversation, playing the part of both Lvov and himself. Because of the importance of this conversation, which Kerensky considers conclusive proof of Kornilov's plot, it is quoted in its entirety:

Conversation over Hughes Apparatus
(Kerensky's Italics)

Kerensky: Good day, General. V.N. Lvov and Kerensky at the apparatus. We beg you to confirm the statement that *Kerensky is to act according to the communication made to him by V.N.*

Kornilov: Good day, Alexander Feodorovich; good day, V.N. Confirming again the description I gave V.N. of the present situation of the country and the army as it appears to me; I declare again that the events of the past days and of those I see *coming imperatively demand a definite decision in the shortest possible time.*

Kerensky as Lvov: I, V.N., ask you *whether it is necessary to act on that definite decision* which you asked me to communicate privately to Kerensky, as he is hesitating to give his full confidence without your personal confirmation.

Kornilov: Yes, I confirm that I asked you to convey to Alexander Feodorovich my urgent demand that he should come to Mogilev [location of headquarters].

Kerensky: I, Alexander Feodorovich, *understand* your answer as *confirmation* of the words conveyed to me by V.N. *To do that* today and start from here is impossible. I hope to start tomorrow. Is it necessary for Savinkov to go?

Kornilov: I beg urgently that Boris Viktorovich shall come with you. Everything I said to V.N. refers in *equal degree* to Savinkov. I beg you earnestly not to put off your departure later than tomorrow. *Believe me, only my recognition of the responsibility of the moment urges me to persist in my request.*

Kerensky: Shall we come *only* in case of an outbreak, of which there are rumors, or in any case?

Kornilov: In any case.

Kerensky: Good day. Soon we shall see each other.

Kornilov: Good day.

Note that the only thing which Kornilov confirmed was his demand that Kerensky come to Stavka. Since Kerensky was the interrogator, one must wonder why he was not more precise in his questioning. For example, why did he not simply read off the conditions written down by Lvov and ask Kornilov to confirm or deny each of them? The most likely reason is that Kerensky now believed that Kornilov planned to double-cross him. Kerensky, despite his willingness to use Kornilov to suppress the Left, had assumed that he (Kerensky) would continue to head the government. Now, on the basis of Lvov's report, it appeared that Kornilov meant to place himself at the top. Kerensky did not intend to relinquish power, and Lvov's report presented him with an opportunity to turn the tables on Kornilov. The Prime Minister deliberately employed vague phraseology when questioning the General so that Kornilov would have no opportunity to deny a conspiracy. Kerensky did so realizing that a straightforward denial on Kornilov's part would make it difficult to gather support of the Provisional Government to act against what Kerensky now chose to regard as a plot against the duly constituted authority — himself. To put the matter somewhat crudely: "Kerensky seized the most propitious moment, in order not to be eaten by Kornilov, but on the contrary to devour Kornilov himself."

The burden of providing proof of Kornilov's guilt rests with Kerensky. His conversation of September 8 with Lvov and his subsequent communication with Kornilov over the wireless do not justify the accusation that Kornilov planned to overthrow the Provisional Government. Kerensky's decision to treat Kornilov as a rebel was unwarranted on the basis of the evidence available to him at the time.

Yet Strakhovsky concludes from the foregoing that Kornilov did not intend to overthrow the Provisional Government. This is not quite true, for Kornilov did intend to act unilaterally to suppress the radicals in Petrograd — a step that was in open defiance of the Provisional Government when it was planned and that undoubtedly would have toppled the government, as Kornilov was surely aware. But Kerensky had no knowledge of Kornilov's plan. As early as August 19, Kornilov instructed his Chief of Staff, General Lukomsky, to concentrate the Third Corps in the areas of Nevel, Novye-Sokolniki, Velikie-Luki, within convenient striking distance by railroad of both Moscow and Petrograd. After some prodding by

Lukomsky, Kornilov gave as his reason the anticipated Bolshevik insurrection of September 10-11 and intimated he was prepared to act to suppress it without the consent of the Provisional Government. On September 3, I.P. Romanovsky, Quartermaster General of the Chief of Staff of the Supreme Commander-in-Chief, signed an order to distribute hand grenades to divisions that were to seize Petrograd from the south. By September 6, before the termination of Savinkov's conversations with Kornilov, the three cavalry divisions composing the Third Corps were concentrated at their respective positions.

Thus we see that those who portray Kornilov as an innocent lamb duped by Kerensky are guided more by feeling than by fact. Kornilov's plan to march unilaterally against the Bolsheviks would have led to confrontation with and probably the overthrow of the Provisional Government. But Kornilov altered his plans following the visits of Savinkov and Lvov. He now felt certain that the Provisional Government would work with him, and for the first time the prospect of a peaceful and legal strengthening and reorganization of the government seemed probable. That Kornilov believed this is evident from the telegrams he sent to Miliukov, M.V. Rodzianko, and other public leaders, inviting them to Stavka on the morning of September 10 to discuss the question of a collective dictatorship. The fact that Kerensky was invited one day earlier suggests that Kornilov wanted to come to terms with him, amicably if possible, by pressure if necessary, before he met with other political leaders. Moreover, on September 9, before he received his note of dismissal, Kornilov sent the following telegram to Savinkov: "Corps will be concentrated in the surroundings of Petrograd the evening of the 10th. I request that you declare Petrograd under martial law September 11." Surely this was an absurd request for someone planning a conspiratorial seizure of power.

There is some evidence that Kerensky regretted his precipitate action in dismissing Kornilov on September 9. For example, he hesitated publicly to denounce Kornilov as a mutineer and agreed under pressure from his ministers to delay publication of such a report until after new conversations were held with the generals at headquarters. As late as the evening of September 9, Kerensky agreed to the request of the League of Cossack Troops that a deputation from that body should be permitted to go to Mogilev with the object of mediating between the government and the supporters of Kornilov. Kerensky was also under strong pressure from Savinkov, Miliukov, Alekseev and Tereshchenko to negotiate. As late as 4 A.M., September 10, Kerensky hesitated to denounce Kornilov as a rebel. This suggests that he still had doubts about the alleged coup theory. At this time, Tereshchenko learned that earlier in the evening Nekrasov,[6] without Kerensky's permission, had dispatched a message denouncing Kornilov as a traitor. The Minister for Foreign Affairs hurried to inform Kerensky of what had transpired. Kerensky, who at the moment was conversing with Alekseev about negotiating with Kornilov, was shocked. Urged on by Alekseev, Tereshchenko, and Savinkov, Kerensky hurried to the Winter Palace to try to delay publication of the message. But it was too late. Nekrasov's arbitrary action made any compromise between Kerensky and Kornilov impossible. It informed the country for the first time of the accusation that Kornilov had mutinied and was marching against Petrograd. And it caused Kornilov, in a proclamation to the people, to break openly with the Provisional Government.

Was there a Kornilov revolt? The answer is yes. As we have seen, Kornilov was prepared to march against the Bolsheviks without the support of the Provisional Government. His plans were drawn up in the third week in August, and preparations were completed by September 6. But after his conversation with Savinkov, Kornilov was convinced this operation had the government's blessing. He was especially pleased at

---

6. Leading Cadet politician and assistant to Kerensky in the Provisional Government — Ed.

the request to send a corps to Petrograd, since this relieved him of the onus of doing so illegally. Lvov's visit further persuaded him of Kerensky's readiness to surrender power, and the latter's willingness to come to Stavka, as transmitted by telegraph, confirmed this impression. But Kornilov was always prepared to act on his own if need be, and in disobeying Kerensky's order of dismissal on September 9, he was merely returning to his original plan.

On Kerensky's side, the picture is not so clear. After initially opposing Kornilov, by August 30 he appeared willing to work with the General. He sent Savinkov to Stavka in the first week of September to work out the final terms. The visit to Lvov on September 8 panicked Kerensky, for he now believed that he and Kornilov interpreted their agreement differently — as part of the plan, Kornilov expected to replace Kerensky as head of the government, the last thing Kerensky intended. Doubly fearful because of his own request for a corps to be sent to Petrograd, Kerensky, on insufficient evidence, accused Kornilov of planning to overthrow the government. In effect, Kerensky was now acting against a "legal" conspiracy designed to strengthen the government and suppress radicalism in the capital, a "plot" which his own negotiations with Kornilov through Savinkov had made possible. He probably felt that to bolster his government he had sold himself out on poor terms to Kornilov. Now he wanted to renege on a bad deal. Lvov's intervention gave him this opportunity. Kerensky also may have concluded at this late date that the enterprise had little chance of success in view of the widespread opposition from the Soviets and moderates it was sure to arouse, and that he should pull out to avoid being purged along with Kornilov.

As the "hostage of democracy," the chief link between the Soviets and the bourgeois members of the Provisional Government, he was the symbol of coalition government. Moreover, since his sympathies lay with the moderate Left, Kerensky hesitated to enact stern measures which might unduly excite public opinion, even though he recognized the necessity of halting the disintegration of the army. Thus Kerensky vacillated, wanting to support Kornilov's program, yet fearing it might lead to a dictatorship of the Right. His conduct at the Moscow State Conference and his handling of the Lvov episode suggest that not only was he physically exhausted but he was laboring under enormous mental strain as well. In any case, the rationale of the original conflict with Kornilov disappeared. The struggle which ensued was waged between men and not ideas. The questions of army discipline, of the Bolshevik menace, of reform in general became secondary. In their place, stood a new question: Who would rule Russia — Kerensky or Kornilov? History answered neither. For the Kornilov Affair was the prelude to Bolshevism.

# II. SOCIAL REVOLUTION AND BOLSHEVIK INSURRECTION

*John L. H. Keep*

## REVOLUTION IN THE FACTORIES

John Keep (1926- ) is professor of Russian history at the University of Toronto and, among other works, the author of *The Rise of Social Democracy in Russia* (1963). His account of labor's impact on the revolution stresses the spontaneous development of a sweeping attack on the capitalist organization of industry and the possibilities this situation offered the Bolshevik party for the manipulation of worker revolutionary organizations.

THE COLLAPSE OF tsarism was the signal for militant action on a hitherto unparalleled scale by an ever-growing segment of Russia's labour force. The sudden disappearance of the old regime raised intoxicating hopes of a new golden age, or at least of a dramatic improvement in living standards. To most ordinary working people the new freedoms were meaningless unless accompanied by immediately tangible economic benefits. There was a widespread conviction that the upper classes generally, and industrialists in particular, had done well out of the war and that now wage-earners had a moral right to demand greater equality and social justice. If this demand were frustrated, the fault was assumed to lie with the egoism of the privileged groups. Arguments in favour of moderation were suspect, whether they stemmed from considerations of national interest or of economic rationality.

In this way a gulf began to yawn between the country's educated minority, whose attention was focused on political problems, and the popular masses, especially in the towns, who became increasingly preoccupied with the struggle to protect or advance their material interests. During the earlier part of 1917, at any rate, very few ordinary workmen thought about destroying the "capitalist" social order: such abstract questions concerned only a small number of activists subject to the influence of the radical intelligentsia. Of a hundred petitions which industrial employees submitted to various central authorities in March 1917, scarcely any mentioned socialism: but 51 per cent of the petitioners demanded a reduction of working hours, 18 per cent called for higher wages, 15 per cent complained about poor hygienic conditions in their place of employment, and 12 per cent claimed rights for the committees which had sprung up spontaneously in many enterprises. The analyst of these data concludes reasonably enough that at this juncture "the workers sought to ameliorate their condition, not to transform it." Yet the scope of their demands quickly escalated until their cumulative force amounted to a call for a new system of industrial relations, an im-

Reprinted from John L.H. Keep, *The Russian Revolution: A Study in Mass Mobilization*, pp. 67-71, 74-80, 84-87, 90-95, with the permission of W.W. Norton & Company, Inc. Copyright © 1976 by John L.H. Keep.

plicit challenge to the basic principles of a free-enterprise market economy. Even prosperous and well-disposed firms faced collapse if they were to concede all the demands put forward simultaneously on behalf of their employees. What was more significant, these demands could not be wholly satisfied by any of the parties or groups active in Russian political life during 1917: even the Bolshevik programme did not do justice to the almost apocalyptic hopes engendered among a broad segment of their clientele. These sentiments did, however, lend themselves to exploitation for other purposes.

Any account of the development of the Russian labour movement in 1917 is liable to be somewhat impressionistic. There are two main reasons for this. First, the economic breakdown, which assumed catastrophic proportions in the latter half of the year, led to a near-collapse of the statistical services. The fragmentary information collected at that time is of doubtful reliability. In the second place Soviet historical writing on the subject suffers from a strong element of ideological bias. Nevertheless a few general points are clear enough. Chronologically, peaceful forms of protest gave way to more violent and aggressive actions as the year wore on; geographically, the main focal points of unrest were Petrograd and the Northwest, then Moscow and the Central Industrial region; sociologically, the movement was led by workers in larger factories, who were most amenable to organization for militant ends, while those employed in transport, distribution, clerical or service occupations tended to be more modest in their demands. To some extent the distinction between skilled and unskilled men coincided with that between moderates and radicals, but this was not a golden rule. Workers in metallurgical plants fulfilling defence contracts, who were one of the best-paid groups in industry, assumed a vanguard role. The explanation for this lies in their eagerness to renounce their close involvement in what seemed to them a disastrous and senseless war.

We may consider first the actions taken by labour to press its sectional claims and then turn to the organizational structure which political leaders and activists built in an attempt to bring this largely spontaneous popular movement under their control.

The demand for an eight-hour day had an almost sacramental character for the more politicized elements. No sooner had the Petrograd strikers returned to work, in most cases within three days of the tsar's abdication, than men in several of the city's factories decided to lay down their tools at the end of each eight-hour shift. Their example was infectious. A similar development had occurred after the general strike of October 1905. At that time the employers had offered stout resistance and compelled the men to abandon their campaign. Now the situation was different. Some managers had sound economic reasons for curtailing production; others hoped that concessions on this point might demonstrate the merits of social harmony and defuse a potentially explosive situation. Accordingly on 10 March the Petrograd industrialists' association, after discussions with a delegation from the soviet led by Gvozdev, agreed to the immediate introduction of an eight-hour working day. Since the accord provided that this should not lead to any diminution of pay, this was equivalent to an automatic wage rise proportionate to the reduction in the work load. Overtime was to be regulated by agreement with the factory committees..., which thereby received explicit sanction. These organs were to be established in all enterprises and were entrusted with wide powers. Conciliation boards were also to be set up at various levels to settle disputes. Rather more to the point was a provision in the agreement prohibiting "the removal of foremen and other administrative officials" by arbitrary action from below. Instances of this practice had already caused alarm in entrepreneurial and government circles. Five days later the eight-hour day was introduced in munition plants operating under the control of the War Ministry's Main Artillery Department. The order was signed by Guchkov, who on succeeding to the post of War minister took a liberal line of which he evidently soon repented.

The action of the Petrograd employers, however comprehensible from the standpoint of political tactics, was of dubious wisdom. It undercut the position of their colleagues in Moscow and other centres, who not unreasonably held that a matter of such importance in the country's social and economic life should be the object of legislation by the central government. These men soon found themselves under heavy pressure to make similar concessions. Since entrepreneurial associations were still but feebly developed, individual manufacturers were often obliged to capitulate to demands on this issue presented by their work-people or on their behalf. In Moscow the soviet decided to introduce the eight-hour day in all enterprises in the city by direct action as from 21 March. Some firms had already introduced it, voluntarily or under pressure, and the soviet explained that it did not want to be left behind by events. By the end of April the eight-hour day had been introduced in practice, if not always with full juridical force, in large enterprises throughout the country. The Soviet historian Volobuyev comments with some justice that this victory "strengthened the workers' confidence in their strength" and helped to radicalize the attitude of many thousands of men and women who had hitherto been indifferent to politics, although one may query his assertion that it was achieved in the teeth of stiff opposition by the employers.

The latter complained loudly that a shortened working day was a luxury which Russian industry could ill afford, especially so long as the war continued. Unfortunately there is no reliable way of measuring the eight-hour day's actual impact on labour productivity or company profits. However, it is plain that — along with unofficial "go slows", absenteeism and other infractions of industrial discipline — it contributed to the difficulties which many concerns experienced in making ends meet. Within a few months a considerable number of enterprises had been forced to close and part-time working had been introduced in many others.

This was part of a larger problem: the rapid increase in the wages bill that entrepreneurs now had to pay as a consequence of inflationary settlements, many imposed on them under duress. This pressure seems to have been most intense in the first three or four months after the collapse of tsarism; from July onwards, although nominal wages continued to rise by leaps and bounds, their value in real terms sank so fast that the employers had no grounds for complaint on this particular score. Their preoccupation was now simply to keep production going at all in the face of acute shortages of fuel and the breakdown of the transport system, and to sell enough goods at rapidly inflating prices to meet current expenses. Few succeeded in doing so; the overwhelming bulk of industrial enterprises that continued to function operated at a deficit and had to draw on basic capital to survive at all. . . .

Violence was a familiar feature of the industrial scene in 1917. The most 'normal' form of conflict was of course the strike, which might well be accompanied by coercive acts of one kind or another: destruction of property, assaults on managerial personnel or threats to the security of anyone deemed hostile to the militants' cause. The factory inspectorate was unable to keep an accurate record of the incidence of strikes, and its figure of 3,823,000 working days lost between January and September, as compared with over 4.7 million in 1916, is clearly an underestimate. Of these disputes between two-thirds and three-quarters were said to be non-economic in nature. A Soviet student of the question has claimed that the monthly number of *strikers* (a less reliable indicator) rose from 35,000 in April to 175,000 in June, and then climbed to 1.1 and 1.2 million in the months of September and October respectively. These calculations owe something to an ideologically inspired compulsion to present the labour movement as becoming progressively more militant and better organized (under Bolshevik leadership, of course). They do not take account of the interrelationships between strikes and other forms of protest, whether active, such as the seizure of factories — which made strikes superfluous — or passive, such as the drift of work-people from the cities to the countryside. The strike weapon lost a good deal of its appeal once it became apparent that employers had nothing more to give. Moreover, many employees who found their living standards falling rapidly could not afford to remain absent from their jobs for long.

Especially in the earlier months of the year, strikes were relatively brief. Gaponenko admits that this was because the employers were obliged to yield to pressure from below, with the result that between April and June more than four-fifths of disputes ended favourably for the strikers. It was significant that employers and public authorities responsible for war production were in general readier to grant concessions to their work-people, so that an abnormally high proportion of strikers were tradesmen, artisans and workers in the consumer-goods industries. The nature of the evidence is such that it is often hard to decide whether men were idle because they were on strike or because there was no work for them to do. An increasing number of factories, especially in the textile industry of the central region, were compelled to close their gates, but only in some instances were such closures due to a desire on the employers' part to counter wage demands or discipline the labour force. Radical activists at the time habitually represented such actions as "lock-outs", and this interpretation has become traditional among Soviet historians. However, of 568 enterprises employing 104,000 persons which shut down between March and July, only 79, employing about a tenth of that number, closed because of labour disputes.

The ineffectiveness of strike action enhanced the appeal of more violent measures, up to and including the forcible removal of managerial representatives and sequestration of the plant. In March and April the overwhelming majority of the industrial conflicts reported to the militia involved such disturbances. The proportion of such incidents then fell in relation to the number of strikes, but this tendency was more notable in the Central Industrial region than in the turbulent North-west, the Urals and especially the Ukraine: in the latter area fifty-five strikes and seventy-four other incidents were notified between March and October. In the Urals no less than 145 managers, directors, supervisors and other administrative personnel were dismissed from forty-two enterprises in the four months March to June. These actions were normally the work of militant groups which claimed that they were acting with the consent of the general body of employees. How genuine such claims were could scarcely be determined with any precision at the time, let alone in retrospect. Sometimes the mood in a factory might indeed become so inflamed that the activists could reasonably be said to have the men behind them. In other cases there were significant groups of moderates who disapproved of such actions but were intimidated into remaining silent or absenting themselves from the scene of action....

The practice that best conveys the flavour of industrial relations in Russia during this period is that of thrusting an unpopular individual into a wheelbarrow and trundling him through the factory gates, to the jeers of the assembled crowd; if nothing worse befell him, the victim might then be ducked in a nearby stream or pond. Several instances of this curious and archaic procedure have been recorded from different parts of the country. At the Metal Pipe works in Petrograd this treatment was meted out by men in the forging shop to no less an individual than a deputy of the soviet, an SR by political affiliation, who was also a member of the factory committee set up within the enterprise; before the procession reached the river Neva, men in other departments were alerted and came to his rescue; a fist fight broke out and there were "many victims" (none of whom seem to have been seriously hurt). At Blagodat in the Urals a mining engineer named Domrachev was seized by a mixed crowd of workers and soldiers who "carted him through the streets in a barrow and threatened to take his life"; the ministry of Labour decided to investigate the incident, but the outcome of the inquiry is not known.

All in all this was mild inoffensive stuff, a kind of preliminary sparring before the match began in earnest. Outright seizures of enterprises were still very rare. Where "workers' control" was established, as it was for instance already in March over the factories of Savva and Vikula Morozov at Orekhovo-Zuyevo,[1] it was either with the owner's consent (as in this instance: the Morozovs were well-known for their eccentric left-wing views) or else nominal; often it was seen only as a temporary measure, provoked by the collapse of the existing management, without the revolutionary implications it was to acquire later. For this development the responsibility lay chiefly with the movement to set up enterprise or factory committees.... Of all the *ad hoc* organizations set up by Russia's workers in 1917 these were perhaps the most significant, since they gave expression to their instinctive distrust of authority in any form and their desire to assert control over everything which might affect their conditions of employment. Although the political impact of these committees was slighter than that of the soviets, they were essential adjuncts to the latter in mobilizing popular sentiment. Above all, they were the first mass bodies in which the Bolsheviks were able to strike root.

It was natural that those who organized the informal strike committees which emerged in Petrograd during the February days should seek to perpetuate their existence once the men had returned to work. The first reliable documentary evidence of the establishment of a body with such long-term aims dates from 1 March. It appeared in the Petrograd Cable Works — significantly a metallurgical firm engaged on war work under the control of the military authorities. The latter promptly accepted the men's demands that they be allowed to form an armed militia force, paid by the management, and — in less martial vein — that their committee should run the factory shop, at which foodstuffs were retailed at special prices. In the following days similar committees appeared in a number of other enterprises, with metallurgical-workers in the lead. They began by presenting demands to management on wages, working hours and other matters concerning the internal life of the establishment. Above all the committees sought to win explicit recognition of their right to represent the men in all dealings with management and to control the recruitment and dismissal of personnel — that is to say to establish the principle of the "closed shop". It was but a step from this to demands for virtual veto rights over appointments at managerial level and to naming individuals whom the committee insisted should be dismissed. As early as 5 March certain foremen at the Treugolnik plant in Petrograd were dismissed by the management after they had been accused of "disorganizing production", apparently by insisting on overtime working to which the men objected. At another factory the committee men described their foes sweepingly as "marauders, former servants of the old regime and persons found committing thefts or any other disloyal acts" — the loyalty in question being to the committee and its supporters, of course, rather than to the administration. In four leading Petrograd metallurgical works 174 persons were expelled in this fashion, among them no less than seventy from the Treugolnik plant. The Baranovsky shell factory lost a sixth of its 150 engineers and technicians. Some of the victims who had hitherto enjoyed military deferment were unceremoniously handed over to the local army authorities for despatch to the front, in a procedure reminiscent of that occasionally employed by managers under the old regime.

Initially at least the army chiefs in Petrograd appear to have taken a soft line toward the workers' demands. This must have had some impact upon the readiness with which the manufacturers of the capital as a body concluded the agreement of 10 March providing for the establishment of factory committees in all enterprises. The

---

1. Large textile enterprise to the northeast of Moscow — Ed.

explanation lies partly in the euphoria with which Russian society generally greeted the collapse of the old regime and partly in the military authorities' understandable desire to maintain the flow of armaments at any price. Some manufacturers may have acted in the hope that factory committees would be more tractable than trade unions, which were bound to become linked to left-wing political parties; if so, they were destined to be disappointed.

It was not long before the committees took steps to coordinate their activities, in some cases displaying more energy than the emergent unions. Again it was men in State-owned or State-controlled metallurgical works who took the lead. One may suppose that their activism was prompted by a deep-seated aversion to the bureaucratic forms of management with which they were familiar as well as by a desire to make the best of their employers' relative flexibility. Already on 13 March a meeting was held of representatives of the committees in twelve works subject to the Main Artillery Administration, who set themselves up as a kind of standing conference; it was on this occasion that the question of workers' control over production, which opened up such enticing perspectives, was first formally raised. In the following month they elaborated a detailed "instruction" inspired by syndicalist ideas of industrial democracy. "All administrative personnel, such as works directors, departmental and workshop heads, all technical officials ... and other managerial staff are to assume their duties with the approval of the general factory committee." The latter defined its role as "to control the activity of the works management in an administrative-economic and technical sense". For this purpose its representatives were to be present in all departments of the enterprise and were to have access to all documents, accounts and other official papers. These ideas were rapidly taken up by workers in the private sector of industry, although this was less subject to bureaucratic regimentation and the men had fewer grounds for such extremism. Workers in the Putilov plant were rather slow to form a factory committee, partly it seems because they wanted to hold regular elections, and this took time in such a vast enterprise; however, in April they issued a call for a city-wide conference of factory committee representatives. The idea was promptly taken up by the Bolsheviks, who gave it every encouragement in the hope of winning control over what had hitherto been largely a spontaneous movement. The first factory committees in Petrograd had emerged without external direction and their leaders had no specific political affiliation. Some of them (for example, at the Obukhov arms works) called themselves Socialist-Revolutionaries, but appear to have done so simply because the name of this party seemed to harmonize with their own ideals....

By mid-summer, when the political mood was veering somewhat to the right, the Provisional Government began to take some tardy steps to assert its authority in the industrial-relations field. On 1 July, faced with the threat that one of Moscow's principal metallurgical works, familiarly called the Goujon factory, might have to close because the management could no longer meet increased costs, the Special Council on Defence decided to sequester the plant. Such action was received with mixed feelings in business circles. Some directors and boards of companies, especially smaller ones, welcomed and even requested government intervention, which they saw as a lesser evil than control from below. Others considered that major breaches in the free-enterprise system should be carried out only after discussion with representatives of the interests concerned and should have a limited scope: the old boards should retain full autonomy and merely be required to submit their accounts for periodic inspection. These divisions of opinion were reflected in the regional and national employers' associations, which by this time were beginning to find their feet. On 22 July the council of the Union of United Industry, formed a few weeks earlier by Moscow textile manufacturers, advised its members in a circular letter "to abandon the idea of running enterprises on pre-revolutionary lines" and "to support labour organzations such as the [factory] committees organized... within the limits of the law of 23 April", but to have as few dealings as possible with the soviets, which had no authorized status in law. In this way, it hoped, "the principle of legality might be generally inculcated into the workers' milieu." These ideas were elaborated in a circular to its members dispatched on 22 August, after talks with local representatives of the ministry of Labour. Members of factory committees might be excused from work for a few hours each week to attend to their duties, but unauthorized absence should be punished by an appropriate deduction from pay, and after two weeks' absence such offenders should be dismissed.

Earlier in the month a leading Moscow industrialist and public figure, P.P. Ryabushinsky, inaugurating the second congress of the All-Russian Union of Trade and Industry, delivered a philippic against the government ("a shadow power") and the soviets ("charlatans" and "deceivers of the people"), and called on all those engaged in commerce and industry to rally behind a reinvigorated state power. It was on this occasion that he uttered the phrase, much quoted (usually out of context) at the time and since in left-wing circles, about "the bony hand of hunger" which sooner or later would "clutch by the throat... the members of various committees and soviets, forcing them to come to their senses".

In practice, however, the employers did little to improve the climate of industrial relations, preferring rather to await a positive turn of events in the political sphere. The factory committees, naturally enough, were one of the main targets of their wrath, yet it was scarcely possible, politically or practically, to make them observe the law. There were occasional instances when employers refused them recognition, on the grounds that they were irregularly constituted or had exceeded their powers, or subjected them to petty harassment, such as denial of premises in which to meet, in the hope that this would oblige them to conduct their activities outside working hours, as in principle they were supposed to do. One employers' association carried out an inquiry among its members to discover the scale on which these bodies were being maintained at management's expense: the fourteen firms which replied stated that they had spent about 1.5 million roubles on this purpose between March and July inclusive. Another inquiry in the Urals elicited a figure of 400,000 roubles. Despite these costly irregularities the employers did not launch a general assault upon the factory committees, and ignored various recommendations they received to the contrary....

In the last two months or so before the Bolshevik takeover the factory committee movement spread more widely and became thoroughly politicized. Actions at enterprise level continued but were less significant than measures taken by local leaders, through the city-wide and regional institutions they had established, to support the campaign for "soviet power". It was in this period that "maximalist" elements, as they were generally called at the time, most of whom were close to the Bolshevik party if not actually members of it, took over control of the enterprise-level committees from those who were of more moderate persuasion or had no definite political affiliation. In Petrograd the factory committees served the Bolsheviks as a handy base from which to launch their assault on the moderate leadership of the soviet....

The growing intransigence and aggressiveness displayed by the factory-committee movement enhanced the importance of the para-military formations organized under its aegis. These units are customarily referred to by the colourful name of "Red guards", as they were christened by enthusiasts. However one should not overlook the distinction between them and the workers' militia groups from which they were derived.

The workers' militia, like the factory committees, originated in the armed clashes of February. The revolt of the soldiers in the capital led to acquisition of weapons by a number of working-class activists. From the arsenal alone the insurgents seized 40,000 rifles and 30,000 revolvers. Another 24,000 rifles and 400,000 cartridge were handed over under duress by the Provisional Government's Military Commission between 2 and 4 March. When the men returned to work, some of those with arms took on the function of patrolling factory premises and maintaining order in industrial districts of the city. At first they pursued limited aims of a defensive kind: for example, restraining "hooligan elements" who were liable to get drunk and engage in actions that would discredit the new order. It was not long, however, before they began to direct their energies against suspected "counter-revolutionaries", including of course managerial personnel. The cases of violence discussed above were as a rule perpetrated not by ordinary workmen acting on impulse but by members of these armed bands. They generally referred to themselves as "the militia" or "militiamen"; the word "workers" or "factory" was sometimes attached to distinguish them from the regular militia (civilian police), which on the morrow of the February revolution was placed under the nominal jurisdiction of the organs of local self-government (municipalities, zemstva)....

In Petrograd as elsewhere the relationship between the two formations was a complex and shifting one. Legally, only the latter had any right to exercise police powers. In practice they were obliged to share responsibility with bands of armed men acting at the behest of various unofficial organs: factory committees, trade unions or urban and city-district soviets. Sometimes they took their instructions directly from one or other of the political parties. The relationship between the municipal authorities (or "committees of public organizations") and these unofficial bodies reproduced in microcosm the so-called "dual power", the uneasy coexistence between the Provisional Government and the Petrograd soviet. Some more determined municipal leaders endeavoured to bring local militia groups under closer control by verifying the qualifications of those who had joined them and expelling individuals whose loyalty to the new order was in doubt. Frequently, however, such efforts were hamstrung by pressure from radical elements within the municipal board or in the soviet, so that the regular militia was obliged to tolerate the presence within its ranks of men who made no secret of their subversive intentions.

Appeals for the voluntary surrender of weapons had little or no effect, and the general political and military situation made it impossible to uncover them by force. Sometimes regular militiamen were bribed or threatened into surrendering their arms to their rivals. However, major confrontations were generally avoided. In practice the two systems of police authority contented themselves with mutual surveillance. They spent their days in routine tasks such as guarding buildings while such major problems as catching law-breakers and bringing them to justice were neglected. This opened up tempting opportunities to members of the criminal underworld, who sometimes disguised their activities by adopting political labels.

While the Mensheviks and other moderate elements in the soviets vacillated, generally seeking to effect compromises between the two forces, the Bolsheviks endeavoured to consolidate the workers' militia groups under their own control, to build up their popular support, and to give their activities a more overtly political character. Until the Kornilov affair at the end of August these tasks do not seem to have been given a very high priority by the party leadership, despite Lenin's repeated insistence on their urgency. A.G. Shlyapnikov, the senior Bolshevik in Petrograd at the time of the February revolution, disagreed with certain young hotheads who wanted to make the formation of militia groups the party's chief task and urged them to concentrate instead on propaganda among the troops, whose revolutionary potential in his view was likely to be much greater. This became accepted doctrine on the subject during subsequent months. The Bolshevik Central Committee maintained a network of military organizations concerned almost exclusively with agitation among the soldiers. Furtherance of the workers' militia was in practice left to the party's local organs (especially its committees in the city districts) — or simply to the factory committees wherever these could be relied upon to follow the Bolsheviks' lead.

For such limited purposes as overawing hostile elements within the enterprise, or protecting strikers and demonstrators against possible attack, it was scarcely necessary to form an elaborate paramilitary organization. Local bands of men who possessed arms or had a taste for physical combat were simply called upon to act as the occasion arose. One must therefore beware of attaching too much credence to the high figures sometimes given for the strength of workers' militia units in these early days. The fact remains that in a number of factories groups of several hundred men could be mobilized when required; and in the existing administrative vacuum they were a force to be reckoned with. Moreover, the high rate of turnover among members of these bands — in one Petrograd metal works, out of a cumulative total of 470 militiamen registered between March and July 1917, only ten served the full four months, and maximum membership at any time did not rise above 140 — helped to spread a sense of solidarity. "Thousands of workers were exposed to political propaganda through their daily conversations and learned all sorts of practical knowledge necessary for a revolution." . . .

Until August, at least, it could be said that the average militiaman's intellectual horizons remained bounded by his factory walls. The number of such units, however, grew apace, particularly in the provinces. For example, at the textile centre of Orekhovo-Zuyevo it was resolved in May to set up a militia unit, but to keep the decision secret; three hundred rifles and sixty thousand cartridges were obtained from soldiers stationed nearby. After the July Days, an abortive effort by pro-Bolshevik troops to force the soviet leadership to take power, most militia units were obliged to lie low, and in the Petrograd area some arms caches were uncovered by troops loyal to the government.

It was the "Kornilov affair" at the end of August which transformed the situation. Overnight the militia groups became respected "defenders of democracy", tolerated if not actively assisted by the public authorities. In Petrograd three thousand rifles (out of seven thousand originally promised) were handed over to a self-styled "committee for popular struggle against counter-revolution"; other supplies of weapons were obtained through illicit channels. The soviet now under Bolshevik control, thereupon set about creating an infra-structure of paramilitary organizations. The Putilov works, which claimed two thousand militiamen at the time of Kornilov's "revolt", raised that number to five thousand by October. In Moscow a "central staff" came into being at the beginning of September. Among its twenty-four members were representatives of various left-wing factions, but real power lay with its Bolshevik core. In vain did the moderate elements protest that such measures were illegal. The soviet pronounced in favour of the "immediate arming of the workers". In the Lefortovo district of the city benefit concerts were arranged to obtain money for the purchase of weapons; elsewhere arms and munitions were seized from soldiers on guard duty or acquired in exchange for goods. Militiamen at the Mikhelson factory, who for some months had been engaging in regular military training in open country outside the city, organized a raid on a weapon depot which yielded a haul of 120 rifles, 200 revolvers and 24 boxes of cartridges.

In all this feverish political activity the modest original aims of the workers' militia units were forgotten. Established with the object of self-defence against instigators of *pogroms*, or in the hope of forcing employers' hands in industrial strife, they developed into the military arm of a single political party which made no secret of its intention to seize State power by insurrectionary means. Many ordinary Red guardsmen, and also members of the factory committees, will scarcely have been able to comprehend the import of this transformation. Driven to near-despair by the economic crisis, their nerves kept on edge by incessant propaganda, they responded uncritically to the appeals of a party that promised untold blessings once "soviet power" had been achieved. They had acquired a taste for violence on a limited scale, and the insurrection seemed likely to be an easy affair. Small wonder that considerable numbers of working men — and even a few women too — committed themselves to the active or passive support of these bands. One recent analyst has estimated their total size on the eve of the October revolution at between 70,000 and 100,000. Of these, some 15-20,000 were in Petrograd or its environs, about 10-15,000 in Moscow and the Central Industrial region, and roughly the same number in the Ukraine. Not all these men carried arms, and their discipline was poor. As a military force they were much less important than the mutinous soldiers. Yet together with the latter they were strong enough to overawe opponents who had lost the will to resist.

*Lazar Volin*

# THE TRIUMPH OF THE PEASANTRY

Lazar Volin (1896-1966) was one of the leading Western authorities on Russian agriculture, serving for many years as chief of the East European Branch of the U.S. Department of Agriculture. In his opinion, once the tsarist regime had fallen the peasants were determined to appropriate, either by peaceful or by violent means, the estates held by landlords and even large farms worked by enterprising peasants. When the Provisional Government failed to act quickly, the revolution in the countryside became a "ferocious, primitive, and contagious peasant war."

OUTWARDLY all was quiet on the agrarian front during the war years. Even when revolution broke out in the cities, the countryside remained at first so calm that the agrarian question, which had played such a crucial role in Russian politics before the war, was not even mentioned in the first public appeals and declarations issued by the new Provisional Government. There was, as several writers have suggested, an inevitable time lag in the reaction of the villages to the ferment in the cities, owing to the slow pace at which news had to travel in that pre-radio age. This lag was accentuated by the wartime mobilization, stripping the village of its most active elements. Still, the rural calm was deceptive. Soon after the overthrow of the tsar, the peasantry began to make itself heard. Disturbing reports of peasant unrest and direct action against the landlords arrived at the capital. The new liberal Minister of Agriculture, A.I. Shingarev, was preoccupied with food-supply difficulties and was fearful that

From Lazar Volin, *A Century of Russian Agriculture: From Alexander II to Khrushchev* (Cambridge, Mass., 1970), pp. 120-132.

agitation over agrarian reform might interfere with spring sowings. He was reported as wanting to guarantee producers against losing the fruits of their harvest. Accordingly, on March 9, 1917, the Provisional Government responded to reports of peasant disturbances in Kazan province by ordering them suppressed and the instigators prosecuted.

But the people who knew the villages best were well aware that a revolt could be forestalled only by convincing the peasants that a comprehensive agrarian reform was in the offing. The council of the Moscow Agricultural Society urged the government to announce that it would immediately begin active preparation for such a reform "in the interest of the working peasants"; at the same time, the peasants should be cautioned against any "destructive action directed at the estates as being clearly contrary to the national interest, particularly in wartime." There were others, such as the influential populist and future Minister of Food A.V. Peshekhonov, who urged the government to make haste in settling these problems. "If these questions are not solved immediately, anarchy will result and, as a consequence, the kind of agrarian order for which all the democratic parties are striving will not emerge."

On March 17 the Provisional Government issued its first appeal to the peasant population. It stated that the land question must be solved not by force but by legislation to be passed by the people's representatives. Such legislation would require extensive preparation involving the gathering of considerable data. "The government considers it an imperative duty to complete promptly the preparatory work on the agrarian question so as to present all the materials and information to the people's representatives." More than a month passed before the Provisional Government announced, on April 21, its decision to set up land committees. The Main Land Committee, headed by a well-known economist and populist sympathizer, A.S. Posnikov, had a cumbersome organizational structure and was heavily slanted in its makeup toward political moderation. It was charged with the task of drafting the agrarian-reform legislation. The local land committees also had some vague administrative functions. In a new appeal to the population, issued when the committees were announced, the government again called upon the peasants to refrain from arbitrary action, "to wait peacefully ... for the Constituent Assembly, which will find a just solution to the land question and will establish a new agrarian order." The appeal also sought to reassure peasants in the armed forces that "in their absence and without their participation no decision will be made regarding the land question."

The government's pronouncements indicate that it had chosen a Fabian course of action in the matter of agrarian reform. It stuck to this course until the end of its short life, even in the face of rapidly developing revolutionary emergencies and despite repeated warnings and proddings from its Socialist Revolutionary Minister of Agriculture, Victor Chernov, and from the land committees. Only a few palliative measures were adopted by the Provisional Governmen in the summer of 1917 — such as the prohibition of private land sales (this was urgently needed to break up growing land speculation). Also the Stolypin land-tenure laws were suspended. With these exceptions all significant action was deferred, according to the standard formula, until the convocation of the Constituent Assembly, which was supposed to settle everything. The calling of this body was first delayed by the Provisional Government until the autumn, then September 17, 1917, was set as the date. Then on August 9 the elections were postponed until November 12 and the opening until November 28. In a more normal period such delays might not be objectionable, but these were anything but normal times. The Provisional Government and democracy were both swept away by the Bolsheviks before the elections could be held. Meanwhile, twenty-four commissions and subcommissions under the Ministry of Agriculture had been working "ceaselessly" to prepare a detailed plan of land reform and organization. This work was interrupted by the October Revolution, and a draft of the new agrarian legislation was never completed. When it is recalled how much work had already been done in this field by various government commissions and agencies, by the zemstvos, by political parties and individual scholars, and by the dumas, it seems strange that so much additional toil and time would be needed to prepare such a measure in 1917. One is reminded of the wise dictum of Walter Bagehot, that generalizations must not be postponed until all the facts are gathered. Substitute "laws" for "generalizations" and the dictum is applicable to the situation just described. Even if long preparations were desirable in a less critical period, there was no justification for a delay in an emergency.

A much earlier deadline for agrarian reform could have been set if it had been given high priority. Why was the sense of urgency about the agrarian problem, so characteristic of the liberal and radical parties when they were in opposition under tsarism, absent when they attained power in 1917? This is one of those fateful questions of the Russian Revolution about which we will probably never cease to wonder and speculate. The Socialist Revolutionary Party, which with its massive peasant support became the main pillar of the Provisional Government, has been particularly criticized in retrospect for the delay in agrarian reform. But it is essential to keep in mind the central fact that Russia's revolution occurred in the midst of a great war. It is true that the ardor with which the war was supported by the coalition parties diminished as one moves along the political spectrum from right to left. By the same token, the attachment to the slogan, "peace without annexation and reparation," was strongest among the rightist groups. But what weighed most heavily in favor of reform postponement with the right wing (the Cadet Party), and probably a considerable part of the center, was the fear that land reform would disrupt the prosecution of the war and worsen the precarious food situation. It cannot aid that this apprehension was unjustified. On the contrary, there was a "clear and present danger" that a drastic redistribution of land, carried out during the war, would have a detrimental effect on production, especially commercial production, and thus further strain the food-supply situation. Equally important was the possible adverse effect of land redistribution on the morale of soldiers at the front. It was feared that, no matter what the government assurances might be, the soldiers would suspect that in a general redistribution their interests would be overlooked or disregarded.

Postponement of the agrarian reform until the end of the war seemed the path of wisdom. To this was added the hope of political moderates that, with the passage of time, the strong passions aroused by the revolution would subside and that it would be possible to adopt agrarian legislation less radical in tenor and less disturbing to the national economy. All this would have been very well were it not for the dangerous state of the peasants' mood, the mounting agrarian unrest and tension in the summer of 1917, cleverly exploited by Bolshevik propagandists. The Provisional Government failed almost to the very end to take seriously or, at any rate, to do anything decisive about this danger until it got out of control. There can be no certainty but it is possible that a land reform, less disturbing to agriculture than a peasant revolt, might have been effected if the Provisional Government had acted early and energetically enough.

Peasant unrest was manifested in the immediate demand for land, voiced in the congresses of peasant deputies in May and in direct action by the impatient and irate peasants, who would brook no delay in what they considered the payoff of the revolution. They were afraid that the landlords would meanwhile skim off the cream of their estates. The peasant attitude is typified by a conversation overheard in a village in Smolensk province: "Well, Nicholas was overthrown without the Constituent Assembly; why can't the nobles be driven from the face of the earth without it?" As in 1905, jacqueries, pillage, seizure of land and other property of the landlords, strikes, and, at the very least, nonpayment of rents became common in the summer and early autumn of 1917. The well-publicized fact that numerous commissions organized by the government were toiling hard over new agrarian legislation had no effect on the disturbed peasant masses. Lenin's demagogic exploitation of the peasant movement for Bolshevik purposes made the situation worse, but it was common for the democratic parties at the time to underestimate the Bolshevik threat. Thus the dilemma in which the Provisional Government was caught was not merely that of external war as against agrarian reform, but also of agrarian reform as against internal war.

A struggle was taking place within the cabinet between Prime Minister Lvov, the proponent of the status quo, and Minister of Agriculture Chernov, who vigorously advocated immediate land reform. Prince Lvov's invocations to local authorities to use force in re-establishing law and order in the countryside were mostly empty words. The weak government lacked the power needed for such purposes. Attempts to use military force, resulting for the most part in peasants pitted against their more rebellious brothers, ended largely in fraternization between armed and unarmed peasants. Furthermore, the local land committees, close to the villages, were as a rule unsympathetic to what seemed to them the standpat attitude of the government. On occasion they even came into open conflict with the central authorities, which sometimes led to arrests. The Main Land Committee also became alarmed about the gravity of the situation and on August 3, 1917, addressed through its chairman, Posnikov, an appeal to the Provisional Government for a speedy enactment of land reform.

Prince Lvov finally felt the government in disgust; but the new Kerensky cabinet did not follow the course advocated by Chernov and the land committees. Considering any further participation in the cabinet futile, Chernov resigned shortly after the departure of Lvov. But as an influential leader of the then powerful Socialist Revolutionary Party and a gifted publicist, Chernov continued his campaign for immediate agrarian reform. His successor as Minister of Agriculture, S.L. Maslov, who was appointed to this post early in October 1917, also pressed for immediate reform, though on more moderate lines. On October 20 a conference of ministers under the chairmanship of Maslov began considering his proposed draft for agrarian legislation. Its key feature was the setting up of a provisional reserve of land for leasing to poor peasants, pending the settlement of the land question by the Constituent Assembly. This reserve was to consist of (1) private estate land that had been leased for no less than three of the previous five years; (2) all state and crown land; (3) private estate land that had been cultivated during the previous five years entirely with the aid of peasant draft power and implements; (4) land taken away from its owners or leaseholders because of a threatened serious decline in value or its remaining unseeded; (5) land for which leases had expired; (6) land voluntarily transferred to the reserve. Finally, even estate land cultivated by the owner with his own draft power and implements could be expropriated, provided: it was found by the land committee that a severe shortage of land existed among peasants in the community; surplus manpower to cultivate the land on the basis of noncapitalist family farming was available; and productivity of land transferred to peasants would not be greatly impaired. An adequate holding had to be left to the estate owner for the needs of his household, employees, and livestock. Rent was to be charged for the leased land from which local and national taxes were to be deducted and the remainder paid to the owner. The land reserve was to be administered by the local land committees, which were to be authorized to reduce excessive rents and otherwise to protect the interests of the peasants.

This law, which the Kerensky government was discussing during the last days of its life, might have satisfied the peasants in June; but it was too late and too little in October. It fell far short of the demands of the dominant socialist parties for nationalization or socialization of all estate land without compensation to the owners. The Socialist Revolutionary Party was bitterly taunted for its proposed draft by Lenin.

Right after the Revolution, in March 1917, there were reported for the whole of Russia only 49 cases of peasants who took direct action against the estates. But in April the number of cases jumped to 378 and in May to 678, affecting 174 and 236 districts respectively. In June, with 988 cases in 280 districts, the agrarian unrest reached its first peak. It declined during the harvest period in July and August, with 957 and 760 cases respectively. The tide rose again in the last two months before the Bolshevik coup, in September to 803 and in October to 1169 cases. There could be no question that the young Russian democracy was being confronted with a sweeping peasant revolt that gained in violence with the passage of time and was no less formidable because of its unorganized character. At first the peasants were engaged largely in tactics of "disorganization," making existence for the estate-owners and managers unbearable through a succession of petty acts of interference, noncooperation, and sabotage. Although acts of violence also occurred at this stage, they were sporadic as compared with the later months when arson, pillage, forcible seizure of property, and even murder of estate owners and their agents assumed wide proportions. Here is one such episode from the province of Tambov in central Russia:

> At the meeting the peasants split into two groups. One proposed to take the estates from the nobles in an orderly way and divide up all the property proportionately among the population, but to preserve the gentry's buildings for cultural purposes. The other group proposed to burn down all the estates ... "By being orderly," they said, "we shall never drive the nobles from the estates." ... During the night of September 7-8 a sea of conflagrations swept over the estates of our county. On the morning of September 8 along the road to the village crowds of people were straggling with stolen property: some with wheat, others with a bed, cattle, or a broken armchair.

There was an incident in Chernigov province in northern Ukraine. On the estate of the former Marshal of Nobility Sudienko, "the stock, equipment, furniture, etc., were divided by the peasants, each taking whatever he could. The land was divided among the peasants, and all the buildings burned down. In the mansion house there were many historical treasures and an enormous collection of books, which the peasants tore up to roll cigarettes."

In their violent attacks on the estates the peasants did not spare, as a rule, the good landlords, those who were known to be kind and helpful to their village neighbors. For instance, the estate of a well-known philanthropist, S.S. Ushakov, in the Kozlovsk district of Tambov province did not escape pillage despite the fact that Ushakov had built an excellent school and was generous with financial assistance to peasants in need. Yet his neighbors joined the mob from other villages in staging the jacquerie. "All furniture was removed from the manor and immediately divided up among the new owners. After that, the manor was set on fire from all sides. The fire spread to other buildings, and within an hour there remained only the pitiful ruins of a large, progressive estate. Even the apiary was destroyed by the mob." Peasant violence often spread out in a chain reaction; during the night of September 11, 1917, for example, thirteen estates in the Kozlovsk district were destroyed and during the next day four more.

The Provisional Government, as pointed out earlier, had no reliable force to cope with the violence, no Cossacks and dragoons as the tsarist government had in 1905. When, for instance, a detachment of soldiers was dispatched to quell the disturbances in the Kozlovsk district, they sided with the rebellious peasants: "On arriving at the scene of the jacquerie, the soldiers usually fired in the air and then hastened to join in the pillage."

Such was the climate of rural Russia during the last two months of the Kerensky government. This was a ferocious, primitive, and contagious peasant war — Pushkin's image of "Russian mutiny, terrible and senseless." In 1917, as in 1905, the worst violence occurred in the black-soil area; the rural sections of the more industrialized non-black-soil region escaped much of the havoc. If any lingering doubt remained as to the urgency and intransigence of the peasants' demand for division of the estates, it should have been dispelled by these events of the autumn of 1917. But this does not mean that the peasants were influenced by such slogans as the demand for abolition of private property and socialization of land. To the peasant rank and file, socialization had at best a purely pragmatic value as a convenient formula for land seizure — it conjured up not the statist giant kolkhoz of the future, but the familiar world of the mir with its egalitarian distribution of land and family farming.[1] And as an immediate proposition this was true even of the Socialist Revolutionary ideologists who had proclaimed socialization at the Congress of Soviets of Peasant Deputies in May and June.

We have already seen how negative and tardy was the response of the Provisional Government to this emergency. It is time now to look at the responses from the other side of the political fence. Little need be said about the right opposition, represented mainly by the Union of Landowners that was organized after the February Revolution. An attempt to attract the upper strata of the peasantry failed. The alliance that Stolypin tried to promote among these elements had not materialized, since the more prosperous peasants preferred to be a part of a united village front or, at best, to remain neutral. The union, therefore, remained composed of the same landowners who had staunchly opposed a moderate agrarian reform ten years earlier. It had not changed its standpat attitude and saw in Minister of Agriculture Chernov its principal enemy. . . .

At the other political extreme was Bolshevism and its undisputed master, Lenin. In the early 1890s, after a brief sojourn in the narodnik camp,[2] Lenin embraced Marxist orthodoxy without ifs or buts. For him there did not exist the qualifications and concessions previously made by Marx and Engels to the Russian narodniks. Lenin also went a step further than the founders of Russian Marxism, Plekhanov and Axelrod. He believed that the Russian village was well along the road of capitalist evolution, with its landmarks of class division and class struggle, leading to the eventual extinction of small peasant farming.

Despite significant tactical deviations, there is no evidence that Lenin ever changed his view. Thus in 1917, before the Bolshevik coup, in addressing a congress of peasant representatives he reiterated this thesis, which in his mind had acquired added significance as a result of the destruction caused by the First World War: "If we continue as in the past with small peasant holdings, even though as free citizens and on free land, we are, nevertheless, threatened by inevitable ruin because the collapse is approaching with every day, with every hour." Lenin never doubted that the victory of the peasants over the landowners would result in a new struggle rather than in harmony. He envisaged two stages in the agrarian revolution: a "democratic" stage, in which the socialists would support the peasants' demand for land; and a "socialist" stage, in which a class struggle on the classical Marxist pattern would take place in the village. For Lenin an alliance with the peasantry as a whole against the landowners was bound to be a temporary marriage of convenience, ending in hostility and divorce. The course of events shows how prophetic was this appraisal.

This theoretical antagonism was early tempered by pragmatic political considerations. Lenin was quick to perceive the opportunity for an alliance of revolutionary workers and peasants in the struggle against Russian absolutism. His strategy in the summer and autumn of 1917 was consistent with the course he had charted during the revolution of 1905. It may be characterized as mollifying the peasants in a bid to gain immediate political power for the Bolshe-

---

1. The *mir* was the traditional Russian village organization, which had charge of village affairs, often including periodic redistribution of farmland among the member families according to the relative number of able-bodied adults in each — Ed.
2. The *narodniks* were populist socialists, forebears of the Socialist Revolutionary party — Ed.

viks, relegating notions of class struggle and the "doom" of small peasant farming to the next stage. Already in April 1917, in a proposed party platform, Lenin was advocating immediate nationalization of land, with its actual disposition left to the local soviets of peasant deputies. The peasants were advised not to wait for the Constituent Assembly and to proceed immediately with the confiscation of estate land. However, the estates should not be divided but run as model farms by the soviets of agricultural workers' deputies. In this we can detect Lenin's doctrine of class division among the peasants, as in his advocacy of soviets of poor ("semiproletarian") peasants and separate factions within the broader soviets of peasant deputies. "Without this, all the sweet *petit bourgeois* phrases of the narodniks about the peasantry as a whole will only serve as a cover for a defrauding of the poor masses by the prosperous peasants, who represent merely one of the varieties of capitalists."

As the summer passed and the peasants became more rebellious, Lenin increasingly stressed a tactical rapprochement with the peasantry. "We are not doctrinaires. Our teaching is not dogma, but a guide to action," he wrote. "The peasants want to retain small farming, distribute the land on an equal basis and periodically equalize the holding. Let them. Just because of this, no sensible socialist will break with the poor peasants... The transfer of political power to the proletariat — this is the essential thing."

This was actually the course followed by the Bolsheviks upon seizing the reins of government. One of their first acts was the promulgation of the celebrated decree "Concerning the Land" on November 8 (October 26), 1917 (henceforth referred to as the Land Decree). According to Miliutin, the first Commissar of Agriculture, though he and Larin had prepared the original draft of the Land Decree, the final formulation belonged to Lenin. It provided for the immediate abolition of the property rights of landlords, with no compensation, and the confiscation of all estates, which were to be administered by the local land committees and the district soviets of peasant deputies, pending the final solution of the land problem. In addition, the decree embodied a summary of instructions ... from peasants to their representatives in a congress of peasant soviets held in the summer of 1917, which had been dominated by the Socialist Revolutionaries. The main points of the document were: private property in land was to be abolished, with consequent prohibition of the selling, leasing, and mortgaging of land; the land was to become the possession of all the people, to be used by those who tilled it; all land was to be turned into a general national reserve administered by the local self-governing bodies, with the exception of special land such as orchards and nurseries (these were to become national or communal property). From this reserve every citizen who wished to engage in farming was entitled to an allotment, but only if he cultivated the land himself and employed no hired labor. The allotments were to be equalized on the basis of a labor or consumption standard or norm, with periodic redistribution depending on growth of population and increased productivity. The form of land tenure was to depend entirely on the peasants themselves. ...

The peasant revolution, even after it was legalized by the new regime into a land reform, remained essentially a grass-roots affair, conducted with little reference to government legislation, which in any event was couched in generalities. Sometimes district authorities even enacted their own legislation; the Syzran district of Simbirsk province, for instance, passed a separate socialization law. The situation was frankly summed up by Minister of Agriculture Sereda, at the All-Russian Conference on Party Work in the Village: "The process of fragmentation, the process of partition of land, occurred to a considerable extent spontaneously ... frequently we found arable land without any hay land, the proper relationship between different kinds of land use disturbed, and implements destroyed."

The peasants divided among themselves not only the estate land, but whatever other property they could lay their hands on. "Everything was divided, including the piano... Large buildings which could not be divided were left without frames, doors, and stoves." This description from one province epitomizes the general situation. Yet there were also peasant communities that were reluctant to proceed with land division without the sanction of a constituent assembly. The reluctance was due not to any lack of desire for additional land, but to a feeling of insecurity over possibly invalid acquisitions. The foreboding was prophetic, since in a little over a decade the right to possess land, in the traditional sense understood by the Russian peasants, was lost under collectivization.

The agrarian revolution of 1917, which may be rightly called a peasant revolution, destroyed beyond possibility of revival the Russian estate system and the landlord class. W. H. Chamberlin has written this epitaph: "Pitiless the Russian agrarian revolution was; but from the peasants' standpoint, it was by no means senseless. The flowering of aristocratic landlord culture had cost them too dearly in toil and sweat. And the very fierceness and brutality which marked their upsurge are in some measure an indictment of the social and economic system which they swept away. It had built no adequate protective dikes; it had not given the peasantry enough education, enough sense of a stake in the land, enough feeling for property to insure itself against a violent collapse." Obviously this is only one facet of the picture, since it fails to take into account the progress made between 1905 and 1914 or the full effect of the revolution on the peasants' welfare, let alone its influence on the nonagricultural sector. The revolution did not stop, as a radical agrarian reform would have stopped, with the driving out of the landlords and the division of their property. Nor, as a rule, did the larger peasant holdings, the individually owned land that had been purchased privately by peasants from the estates before 1917, escape the revolutionary melting pot. This caused particular anguish and bitterness in the villages, which showed a solid front in the liquidation of estate land. As one peasant who lost his purchased land expressed it: "By God, I never thought that peasants would rob each other. And I, the sinner, joined in robbing the princes [estates] and thought the end had come for the gentlefolk, and the peasants would have full reign. And now it [expropriation] even reaches us."...

By the end of 1918, the peasant revolution had accomplished its main objectives. The landlords were driven out, and the estate land and larger peasant farms were subdivided. The official label of "temporary" attached to the revolutionary distribution of land was correct in the perspective of history. But the new land arrangements basically continued for more than a decade, until they in turn were swept away by collectivization.

*Marc Ferro*

# CITIZEN-SOLDIERS IN THE REVOLUTIONARY STRUGGLE

The millions of Russian men serving in the army in 1917 were largely of peasant origin. Their behavior in the revolution, however, was determined by their experience and needs as soldiers, in the opinion of Marc Ferro, director of studies at the *Centre de recherches historiques* of the *Ecole pratique des Hautes Etudes* in Paris, France. Ferro minimizes the disorder in the army, stressing the widespread support in the early months for the Petrograd Soviet and the general desire among the new "citizen-soldiers" for a new-style army and for peace. Support within the army for the extremist program of the Bolsheviks grew as the initial demands of the soldiers were frustrated.

AT THE fall of the tsarist government, there was an outburst of joy among the soldiers at the front that was equaled by those at the rear. The letters and telegrams they sent to the Petrograd Soviet and the Provisional Government divulged their miseries, desires, and aspirations. In this respect they behaved like other sections of the population, but with one difference. For the workers the Soviet to which they appealed was one of two powers born of the February Revolution, the organ of their class confronting the government — but there was no such duality for the soldiers. The majority expressed confidence in the Soviet and considered the government to be merely an executive body; only a small minority declared their confidence in the government or recommended that the two should come to agreement. Besides, the workers were often members of trade unions or political parties which spoke on their behalf. No one spoke for the soldiers except the soldiers themselves. Consequently for most of them the Petrograd Soviet was the only body whose legitimacy they recognized, and it was also their sole means of expression. In answer to its call they had set up committees at company or battalion level (soon to be called soviets), and their representatives took part in debates in the Petrograd Soviet, where they felt at home. The reactions of militant workers and party men confirm this impression. Military representation having evaded the politicals' grasp, they sought to reduce or eliminate it on the pretext that "the soldiers constituted the most counterrevolutionary element of the revolution." Within a few months the soldiers came to realize this and their behavior changed.

In March and April front-line soldiers, like those at the rear, expressed hopes that to some extent reiterated and developed various items of Order No. 1.[1] The soldiers aired grievances against their officers for

---

1. Order issued by the Petrograd Soviet on the subject of soldiers' rights — Ed.

---

From Marc Ferro, "The Russian Soldier in 1917: Undisciplined, Patriotic, and Revolutionary," *Slavic Review*, XXX (September, 1971), pp. 484-497, 500-511. Reprinted by permission of the editor.

57

abuses they had suffered: excessive penalties, acts of violence, coarse language, injustice, and arbitrary punishment. Soldiers were human beings — they would no longer accept humiliating practices such as the use of familiar forms of address and other degrading formulas like saluting and standing at attention. As citizens they demanded the rights that henceforward would be enjoyed by civilians — access to information, right of assembly, petition. Order No. 1 stated that soldiers in the ranks and on active duty were under the strictest military discipline, but that in their private and political lives they could not be denied the rights, possessed by all other citizens, of assembly and debate, information, and political representation. These wishes were constantly reiterated in the great number of resolutions that were intended to transform the entire army statute. To these complaints were added those of the soldiers of all countries. They had lived through a nightmare for more than two years and were old before their time. And who behind the lines appreciated this and could truly judge the extent of their sacrifice? They asked that their living conditions be improved and that the government and General Staff give some thought to their daily existence and to the bad food they were reduced to eating. Then too, remembering the state of penury of their wives and children, often destitute since the mobilization, they asked for higher pay, an increase in the family allowance, and guarantees in case they became permanently disabled and could no longer work and support their families.... The large number of texts proposing modifications of the military regulations, referring to combatants' rights within the nation, or demanding the right of national minorities to have separate military units proves that the fighting men did not expect to return home soon....

Consequently in the minds of the soldiers Order No. 1 and subsequent developments in no way implied "the death of the army" any more than the "denial of discipline."... At most the troops demanded the eradication of a certain conception of discipline. At that time, though they may have held some officers responsible for abuses, they still ascribed the general disciplinary regulations to the autocracy, and it seemed to them that their radical modification by the new regime went without saying. Gerhard Wettig has seen clearly that except for outrages against those who opposed the triumph of the revolution "the soldiers were not conscious of attacking their officers regarding fundamentals; they wanted to participate in the revolutionary movement. It was not in their minds to change the military system but to take part [in all that was to be decided]. If the officers declared their loyalty to the revolution they were acknowledged as legitimately in command and the soldiers became 'loyal' again."

But the reaction of most of the officers made the soldiers realize that the military set-up was an expression of the old regime. Order No. 1 had outraged the officer class, for it struck a blow at their rights of decision and command. The roles were reversed in that the soldiers had dictated a decision, and it was one that had the specific effect of restricting officers' rights. Already some among them considered themselves dishonored for having submitted to the change of government or, on the other hand, for not having taken part in it. Consequently in the eyes of the soldiers the officers identified themselves with the old discipline and by that very fact with the old regime.

No doubt the tradition of obedience to the hierarchy inhibited a good many of the officers so that they could not ignore the directives of the General Staff, which was hostile to any transformation. But when it came to taking soldiers' wishes into consideration concerning the democratization of the army, General Alekseev stated to Guchkov[2] that in his capacity as commander in chief he refused to consider methods which would lead to the destruction of *his* army. He gave the tone, and in spite of all the committees (including officers) and the proposals for declarations on soldiers' rights, from then on

---

2. First minister of war in the Provisional Government, forced to resign in the April crisis — Ed.

many officers thought that any alteration of the rules made under compulsion was an insult to their rank, a slur on their honor, a "blow struck at Russia." The same was true of questions regarding recognition of soldiers' political rights and of the legitimacy of political discussion within the army. . . .

Most officers did not even attempt to support their arguments by recourse to history. To admit that ordinary soldiers were citizens like themselves, to discuss matters in a "committee," on equal terms with them, was intolerable. They believed the soldiers incapable of dealing with problems which they considered strictly within their own jurisdiction. They began to realize with misgivings that they had never pondered the issues now being broached at the meetings, whether those issues were political or merely disciplinary. Protected by an institution as old as the army was, they had never bothered to analyze it or work out its relation to the social and political systems. Besides, they had always shown a complete lack of interest regarding public affairs . . . and they had no idea how to handle general political questions. Even more than in the armies of the other belligerents, Russian officers had lived apart from civilian society, and the first meetings held in March and April brutally revealed their political ignorance, their complete incapacity to deal with questions that some junior officers, noncommissioned officers, or soldiers were able to handle with ease. During the first weeks of the revolution many officers had taken part in political meetings, but they soon withdrew, for their inability to discuss problems of war or peace could have endangered their authority as officers and could have raised doubts about the legitimacy of their right to command. But the wind changed, and one of the first concerns of the General Staff, in August, was to control the discussions and to oblige soldiers to inform their superiors of the subject of their contribution to the debate before taking the floor. They intended next to abolish all political discussion within the army, but the Kornilov affair interrupted this process and brought it to an end.

An important minority of junior officers adopted a different attitude. This group seems to have been composed mainly of sergeant-majors and lieutenants who lived with the soldiers in the trenches and ran the same risks. A kind of "spirit of the front" was able to draw together men who had nothing in common in civilian life. These junior officers and soldiers shared strong feelings of resentment against the General Staff and everyone else who was unaware of the price of their sacrifice — those behind the lines and others who profited from war.

The fact remains, however, that for the great majority of officers — revolution or not — relations with the troops were of the simplest. The soldier was judged by his capacity to obey, to salute, to stand at attention. The salute was the true test of obedience. But after Order No. 1, soldiers no longer saluted as before; nor did they obey as before: "Up till now every time I gave an order the soldiers carried it out; this is no longer done. Invariably one of them, referring to the printed text in his hands, would say, no, this is not done any longer. If I asked to see the text, he would not give it to me."

These were the first consequences of Order No. 1 which the General Staff and the Provisional Government tried to obviate by the device of making the soldiers swear loyalty to the new regime. This oath would allow a revival of the habit of obedience without discussion or comprehension. The soldiers contested this oath with as much vigor as the Soviets and the political parties. They felt that "this was a way to rob them of their freedom." A provincial soviet went even further: "It is the government that should take an oath of loyalty to the soldiers." Some units took the oath, others did not, and that was as far as it went. But the officers were indignant, for they were convinced that without the oath and the salute there would be no discipline, and without discipline, no army. In the face of the enemy, lack of discipline was the equivalent of treason, and from treason to the scaffold was but a short step. This syllogism constituted the entire mental framework of many of the officers. No hatred was involved; rather they felt some pity for those they considered untutored, intoxicated with freedom, and in need of being saved against their will from the effects of a propaganda that might lead them straight to the scaffold.

For no one doubted that "it could not last." But it did, in spite of all the Orders and all the proposed reforms. After the setback of the July Days some cherished the illusion that the period of rot had come to an end and order would once more reign. The officers had shown for some time, as the soldiers and noncommissioned officers of the fortress of Kiev had pointed out, that "they could make no sense of our revolution." Six months after the fall of the tsar, General Ostriansky sent a report to General Headquarters asking what steps were being considered to re-establish the power of the army. According to him, "at all costs preventive measures [sic] had to be taken to revive the habit of obedience in the soldier and so to be able to rescue him from the death penalty. Above all, the practice of saluting should be reinstated, but with modifications. For instance, it could be abolished in railway stations and in the trenches, and the distance could be reduced to forty paces and even to five in certain cases." That same summer a general of the Army of the Caucasus thought that the virtues of obedience could be revived by substituting physical exercise for the gambling and card-playing that were indulged in during off-duty hours. Tired out, the soldiers would not have the energy to disobey. The troops in question were Georgians, Armenians, and Azeris. They mutinied, and the unfortunate officer, for having shown such a lamentable ignorance of psychology, soon died a victim of their brutalities.

In the background there was obviously the problem of peace. But its connection with questions of discipline and officers' behavior was not evident; it came to light only through experience. The soldiers in their petitions did not dare — with some exceptions — to express their desire for peace, no matter how natural, until the appeal of the Soviet on March 14. Before the fall of the tsarist regime it had been a constant theme in their letters and demands. Thus it was that for two to three weeks the soldiers, dreaming only of peace, expressed themselves solely in terms of their patriotic duty....

On the morrow of the fall of the tsar, yearnings for peace were rarely expressed. Like everyone else the troops called for the meeting of a constituent assembly, the setting up of a democratic republic, and a whole series of measures of political and social import, none of them very specific, whose true significance was not yet clear. For the rest they confined themselves to demands bearing on their status as both combatants and citizens, which implied that they did not expect an immediate end to the war. To be sure, their desire for it was undiminished even though they declared their readiness to fulfill their patriotic duty — had they been fully sure about this, they might not have emphasized it so strongly. All the same, on March 4 sailors of the Helsingfors testing grounds "demanded that the government officially approach the German people with a note inviting them to overthrow the kaiser and initiate peace negotiations." Some soldiers informed the Soviet that "for the troops a change of regime betokened the end of the war." On March 10 a group of soldiers of the 202nd Regiment wrote, "As regards the war and its continued prosecution we believe that as long as 'our dear cousin' is at the head of the German nation, any agitation against national defense ... is untimely.... In actual fact the public is weary of it, the misery of the people is beyond measure, and there is no shadow of doubt that it is essential to bring the war to an end. But in order to do so the Soviet and other workers' organizations with authority must take the first steps and make contact with the workers' parties of the allied or enemy powers to hasten the end of the war and conclude peace.... But until then the Russian army must hold its external enemy in check."

This was the feeling of the majority. Still influenced by official propaganda, the soldiers of the Sixth Artillery Park asked the

Petrograd Soviet if those who talked of making peace or who supported the views of workers on strike should not be considered agitators. They were not alone in this opinion. Discussions among Bolsheviks or Menshevik-Internationalists bear witness that on the question of peace, no matter what the proposed attitude, militant workers had the greatest difficulty in talking to the troops about peace. In Russia as in all other belligerent countries a silent antagonism, cutting across class barriers, had for a long time set the men at the front against those at the rear. In the opinion of the soldiers, those behind the lines were all shirkers and profiteers — above all the bourgeoisie and kulaks, but also the workers. The latter especially enraged the soldiers because they had the effrontery to make demands when their lives were not endangered. Undoubtedly the workers led a miserable life, but it was still preferable to the life of the fighting men. Numerous letters from soldiers point out that "while workers complain of working more than eight hours a day, soldiers stay in the cold in trenches around the clock." The sailors felt the same way. Three years of war had given many combatant troops a veteran's mentality. The tsar, priests, and officers were no longer the only ones to identify themselves with Russia — the fighting men did too. Moreover, they refused to admit that the war could be discussed by anyone who had not taken part in it; it was inadmissible to criticize the war if one had not been a participant. Such a right was theirs and theirs alone. To point out the imperialistic nature of the war amounted to questioning the justification for their sacrifice, which was horrible and not to be borne. Witness the demonstration of the disabled in mid-April, when those poor wretches shook their fists at Lenin. His victory would mean that for three years they had been made fools of.

The government's propaganda for "war until victory" thus met with a favorable response. In March it began to have results, and the General Staff, like the bourgeois leaders, were agreeably surprised. In Petrograd, bands of armed soldiers kept a close watch on factories to see that the workers kept on working. Everywhere squads of soldiers marched in procession carrying banners reading, "Soldiers to the trenches, workers to the factories." In Moscow there were difficulties. The intellectuals who controlled the Moscow Soviet mistrusted the soldiers, because in the light of Marxist doctrine they were regarded as peasants and "the most counterrevolutionary element of the revolution." The intellectuals could not see that these soldiers, even if they had never been at the front, behaved *like* the fighting men: in keeping watch on the workers and preventing them from going on strike they believed they were carrying out their patriotic duty.

The militants from the workers' parties found it very difficult to combat this attitude. Leading circles unwittingly helped them by preventing any real transformation of the military system, or democratization, or liberalization.

From then on, among the soldiers, it was a question of what would get the upper hand, their resentment of the General Staff and other officers or their animosity toward the objectors and shirkers in the rear. The militant action of the Soviet representatives tipped the balance; from April onward numerous contingents of soldiers began to declare their solidarity with the working class. A certain ambiguity, however, accompanied the process; for example, to a message of friendship and unity with the working class, the soldiers and citizens of the Irkutsk Thirteenth Hussars added a rider: "But produce arms for *us* so that *your* liberty can be defended."

Naturally the soldiers' animosity was mainly toward the bourgeoisie — all those who advocated "war to the bitter end," "war to the death," and who "fill their bellies while we die of hunger like dogs." *Citizen Soldier* treated this subject with eloquence: "To the end of time caws the crow, scraping clean the human bones on the field of battle! ... what matters to him the aged mother awaiting the return of her son of the octogenarian steering the plow with trembling hands? War to the bitter end, cries the student, who draws thousands to the marketplace and assures them that all our misfortunes are caused by the Germans. Meanwhile his father, who has sold oats at sixteen rubles per bushel, sits in a noisy restaurant where he holds forth on the same ideas. Can the soldiers who line the trenches cry 'war to the bitter end'? No. What they say is very different. Comrade, let those who call for war to the bitter end be sent at once to the front — we will see what they have to say then." This theme, like the rallying cry "the bourgeois to the trenches, the bourgeois to the factories," made its appearance at the start of the revolution in much the same way as the first pacifist slogans.

All this was changed on March 14, when the Soviet called for peace without annexations or indemnities. This initiative removed a weighty obligation: it was no longer irresponsible groups but the revolutionary authorities who were publicly broaching the question of war and peace. Given such official support, messages urging peace abruptly multiplied, often quoting word for word one or another passage from the March 14 appeal. From then on, the struggle for peace (without annexations or indemnities) did not conflict with protection of the homeland. Implementation of this new policy was in the hands of those who enjoyed the new legitimacy, the Congress of the Soviets. The word of the Soviet was the revolutionary truth. It was also that of the country, and thanks to the soldiers it would become that of the government. Like a torrent it swept from its path all obstacles, including Guchkov and Miliukov in the April crisis....

In the rear the analyses and propaganda of anarchist and Bolshevik circles had helped the soldiers, better informed there than those at the front, to work out the relation between the "Miliukov Note,"[3] discussions on the need for active operations, their own transfer to the front, and their replacement by units less well informed politically. This explains the fact that the soldiers at the rear took the initiative in the April days. The appointment of Kerensky, vice president of the Petrograd Soviet, as minister of war, however, bewildered the soldiers. But for many of them active military operations again became legitimate because the supreme revolutionary authority supported them. "Defensist" ideas thus gained ground in May, and Kerensky's tour helped revive the fighting spirit. No doubt, as liberal officers remarked, "only a handful of soldiers were prepared to carry out their military duty even though a great many proclaimed their readiness to do so." May indeed saw the beginnings of the campaign of soldiers over forty asking to go home. Nevertheless the fact remains that a great many units sent messages to the Soviet along these lines, some going as far as to applaud the temporary halting of leaves. Others approved the "rotation of combatants" planned by Kerensky for troops that had not been at the front, a step which at that time might have had the effect of setting the fighting men at loggerheads once again with the troops in the rear. This period was also the most prolific in petitions against deserters.

The June 16 offensive took place; numerous units volunteered, and the troops took a very active part. Even so, for many of the combatants, any decision that resulted in restoring authority to the officers or General Staff was already automatically suspect and counterrevolutionary, whatever the aims supposedly or in fact pursued. This is why a number of units refused to take part in the offensive, while others refused to be transferred and demonstrated against Kerensky and the government's action. It is, therefore, a mistake to attribute the origin of the July Days to the failure of the offensive (and even more a mistake to blame it on the resignation of the Kadet ministers, which occurred only later and served merely to call attention to what had happened). The true cause is found in the fact that an offensive was even attempted. Whether it succeeded or failed, it was the start of a process to resume

---

3. The note issued by the Minister of Foreign Affairs, Miliukov, restating tsarist conditions for peace — Ed.

control of the army and thereafter of society, which ran counter to the deepening of the revolution. Moreover, the decision to take the offensive played its part in a wider context which confirms its significance. The campaign against anarchy, the flare-up of anti-Semitism, and the stirring of nationalist sentiments were all elements that the authorities relied on to be at work among those forces that were reorganizing themselves — the Church, the Cossacks, the Stavka Officers' Congress, the Kadets (considered by the troops to be the officers' party)....

The attack failed, and the General Staff publicly laid the blame for defeat on the Bolsheviks. They waited until the failure of the July Days before adopting this interpretation officially. An official statement on July 7 declared that "our defeat is specifically due to the fact that, under the influence of the Bolsheviks, many soldiers who had received orders went to meetings and did not carry out their orders."

This report outraged the troops that had taken part in the offensive operations; they were being blamed for a failure that had innumerable causes. For instance, in the 506th Infantry Division, specifically mentioned in the report, 2,513 soldiers had been killed or wounded out of 3,000. An annex to a report by General Gavrilov and General Gostov stated that "this defeat was due to the enemy's overwhelming superiority in artillery, two hundred guns against sixteen." But the General Staff stuck to the wording of its communiqué! Since the troops were well aware of the true circumstances of the offensive, their indignation knew no bounds. To them this was one more defeat in a series of defeats that had occurred well before the revolution and in which their comrades had died. The participants blamed the failure on the military heads who had rashly launched the attack. The circumstances are reminiscent of those that led to mutiny in the French army,[4] except that in Russia there was a more deeply rooted distrust and hostility toward the General Staff. Not only were they accused of being capable of sending soldiers needlessly to their death, but they were suspected of having mounted these attacks to rid the army of revolutionary soldiers or for some other Machiavellian purpose. No doubt the General Staff nurtured a few ulterior motives of a political kind, but many officers who had remained close to the soldiers did not share these views. They suffered intensely from their moral degradation and from the general confusion of which they were all now the victims. A letter from a certain Captain Gilbich to his wife has been preserved in the archives. Wounded, he died before finishing it: "Darling, today for the first time for many months I am happy, I am overflowing, with happiness. I am here, caught in the German barbed wire and beside me there is someone I call 'my brother' without being stigmatized as a bourgeois or provocateur."

The military attaché to the commissar of the southwestern front, in a report, added, "The talk is all of hanging and shooting." Moreover the soldiers' distrust and suspicion were directed not only against the officers or the Staff but extended to *all political leaders, even socialists,* with the exception of the Bolsheviks: "People who speak in the name of these parties are received with open hostility. They are not even allowed to speak. The Bolshevik propaganda gains ground, disseminated *not so much by official party militants* [italics added] ... as by the spread of ideas.... Officers have had their horses and their equipment taken away from them." Others, their uniforms. Many were disarmed. In a relentless inversion of the old discipline, "officers were deprived of two days' rations for having favored the offensive."

Thus it was at the exact moment when distrust and hostility toward officers, the General Staff, and political leaders reached a point of no return that the civil and military authorities meant to proceed to take back into their hands control of the army and of society.

The re-establishment of compulsion, the proceedings against the June and July muti-

---

4. Large numbers of French front-line troops mutinied in the summer of 1917 — Ed.

neers, the penalties imposed on them, the reintroduction of the death penalty (which apparently was rarely invoked and even more exceptionally carreied out) were all unmistakable signs. It was a "return to tsarism" for those soldiers "who needed no orders to die." The officers' point of view was different. A staff report noted that "the reintroduction of the death penalty created immediately a very strong impression. Those persons termed Bolsheviks were dumfounded." In general the officers were relieved at this reaction and were optimistic. They mentioned the "sobering" effect of the military tribunals. A general commented with suitable gravity: "The democratization of the army was not in the natural order of things. It was not in line with its function and it had no scientific basis." . . .

During this so-called reactionary period (July-August) the troops no longer confined themselves to demanding the resignation of the bourgeois ministers, the dissolution of the Duma, the transfer of power to the Soviets (not just to the Petrograd Soviet, as in March), the end of the war by concluding a peace treaty without annexations, and release of the Bolsheviks. They refused to put counterrevolutionary orders into effect and frequently protested against the arbitrary powers of military tribunals and, naturally, against the death penalty. For the first time they took up the defense of deserters. An increasing number of them joined in demands for the most radical social reforms: abolition of private property, transfer of land to agrarian committees, workers' control, introduction of a system of compulsory work for the bourgeois, formation of an armed workers' militia, and so forth. A comparison with the petitions recorded in March shows how far they had traveled.

Never had the gap been greater between the determination of the military and political leaders to restore their authority and the soldiers' desire to alter the character of the military institution, to change completely their relationship to the government, and to aspire to a social revolution. The generals who were aware of this phenomenon were extremely pessimistic. By describing all those who opposed the attitude of the generals as Bolsheviks, by prosecuting them before the tribunals, "which was a return to the old regime," the government and General Staff unwittingly credited Lenin's party with a popularity that it owed only partly to its own efforts: "Who are these Bolsheviks? What party do they belong to? . . . The government takes a stand against them, but we do not see what they have done wrong. A short time ago we were against them as the revolutionary government asked us to be, but now, after all its promises — and then nothing — we are slowly going over to the Bolsheviks' side. But send us information." The step had been taken, and in fact from July onward the slogans and key arguments show the Bolshevik influence. Both at the front and among the supporting troops the popularity of Lenin's party was constantly growing, inasmuch as it advocated an immediate peace, the power of the Soviets, and social revolution.

The soldiers were alerted. No longer was there a word or gesture on the part of the government and High Command that was not commented on, discussed, and criticized. The Glazov Soldiers' Soviet commented, "The Moscow Assembly[5] is the first political act of the counterrevolution; it includes only a handful of true representatives of the people"; and their resolution, following hundreds of others, concluded, "the only solution is to entrust all power to the Soviets." So the atmosphere was already extremely tense when the Kornilov affair erupted. As the soldiers of the Berdichev garrison wrote, "rumors of an officers' counterrevolution made everyone nervous." The explosive declarations of General Kornilov and Kaledin[6] brought things to a head. . . . A stream of letters and telegrams expressed the soldiers' fury and their irrevocable hostility to the military authorities in power — "exemplary punishment,"

---

5. The Moscow State Conference, organized by Kerensky in August — Ed.
6. Kaledin, head of the Don Cossack forces, was one of the military leaders supporting Kornilov — Ed.

"heavy penalties for Kornilov and his accomplices." In addition to demanding that Kornilov and Kaledin be brought before the Military Tribunal, the Twelfth Army Soldiers' Soviet and its military committee once again requested the dissolution of the Officers' Union, the replacement of the General Staff, an increase in the powers of commissars, and the appointment of representatives to military committees attached to Stavka and to the minister. All senior officers were to be subject to surveillance.

"The troops will not move in defense of anything except on orders from their political committee." They had no further confidence in anyone. They had been duped, had undertaken an offensive operation doomed from the outset, and now the government was not taking action against the rise of the counterrevolution. Kerensky and the mediators were traitors to the revolution, as the Bolsheviks asserted. Officers and men of the Second Regiment of Vyborg fortress inquired: "The bourgeois have met with no resistance on the part of the socialist ministers. The tension mounts daily, the people can get no satisfaction, and reckless offensives like the June one are launched. Even the Democratic Conference, which hardly represents democracy, has declared its opposition to the industrial classes or the Kadets taking any part in the government. Yet Kerensky continues to negotiate with the Kadets. What is it all about? Is this inertia or is it treason?"

Thenceforward Bolshevization was even more rapid, as innumerable messages testify. Many of the soldiers had continued to have faith in Kerensky even after the June offensive, its failure, and the repression — all blamed on Headquarters and the General Staff. His duel with Kornilov had enhanced Kerensky's reputation, and he was believed in once again. But his fear of breaking with the General Staff, his deep-seated hostility to the Soviets, his preference for negotiations at all costs, and his delusion that he could reconcile the irreconcilable were all factors that induced Kerensky to deal gently with Kornilov and his friends. This attitude had the most drastic results. It alienated for good the sympathy of those who had continued to obey the orders of any institutions yet functioning. The most popular leader abruptly found himself the most despised, for the troops had the feeling that he had betrayed their trust. The cleavage in the army became more pronounced: on the one hand were the troops hostile to any functioning institution, who began to desert unit after unit; on the other were those who remained loyal to the military establishment and the General Staff. . . .

*Conclusions:*

1. It appears, therefore, that during the 1917 revolution the troops behaved quite as much like old soldiers — or veterans — as they behaved like peasants in uniform, the picture painted by Marxist tradition. This is hardly surprising. They were young and the war was their first overwhelming experience, bringing into contact men of widely differing backgrounds. Until summer, the antagonism of the soldiers against the workers was part of the general resentment felt by many fighting men in all countries against those at the rear, the bourgeois, and other shirkers, including workers who had the effrontery to make demands. When the propaganda of the socialist parties enlightened the soldiers on the respective roles of the workers and the bourgeois, their attitude changed. Their slogan was no longer "workers to the workshop, soldiers to the trenches" but "bourgeois to the trenches, bourgeois to the factories." The antagonism between front and rear was replaced by a conflict of another and strictly social kind.

2. The question of peace lay at the heart of all problems. Yet for a few weeks it was not conspicuous, because the troops trusted the Petrograd Soviet to solve it. They identified the Soviet with the revolution and entrusted the latter to the former. So they did not dare advertise their pacifist hopes openly before the March 14 appeal, and when the Soviet condemned fraternization they stopped it; as soon as the Soviet asserted that an offensive was necessary, most of them took part in it. But the policy

of the Soviet leaders had already been called into question. Paradoxically, it was the officers' attitude that helped bring this about; it gave the signal and triggered the alarm. The hostility of most officers toward the democratization of the army and the liberalization of military institutions and their campaign in favor of war to the bitter end and of a resumption of active operations made it clear to the troops that there was a connection between questions of discipline, the army's role in society, the exploitation of patriotic feelings, and the continuation of the war for counterrevolutionary purposes.

Soon, for the soldiers, any action that might restore the authority of the officers was automatically suspect, as for instance with regard to the oath of allegiance and the steps taken to revive "fighting spirit." The Soviet leaders and socialist ministers fell under suspicion in their turn; they shared the discredit which became attached to all leaders, because they adopted the General Staff's point of view regarding the need to re-establish discipline, and later because they supported the June offensive. The damaging identification became firm with the launching of the offensive. So it is incorrect to locate in the failure of the offensive the root of the crisis which overthrew the February regime. The root lay in the decision to launch the offensive. In the opinion of the troops, whether the attack was successful or not, it was the start of an effort to regain control of the army and of society, an effort that ran counter to the success of the revolution, which from then on was associated with the conclusion of peace.

3. A feeling of fellowship united the fighting men. Whole units might swing from obedience to orders to a disappearance of discipline, but individual acts were rare. Desertions should therefore be reconsidered from this angle, for their extent before October has been grossly exaggerated by tradition. More often than not, departures from the front were undertaken by entire units. They were mutinies, not desertions.

In October the great diaspora had not yet taken place. Through consensus of a sort the troops still held the line even if they fiercely declared their desire for peace. For the General Staff, however, which had lost all authority, "there was no more army" except for a few contingents still loyal to the military establishment, chiefly in the artillery, cavalry, and among the non-Russians — and a list of these has yet to be drawn up.

4. Until the offensive, officers called all soldiers who refused to obey their order "Bolsheviks." They thought that by so doing they would discredit Lenin's party in the eyes of the soldiers, but the effect was the opposite. Bolsheviks without realizing it, the discontented soldiers began to take an interest in the party's propaganda. It was the only party that approved the soldiers' actions, and the course of events had not ceased to prove their predictions right. Gradually the troops adopted their slogans, and from mid-July onward Bolshevization of the army proceeded apace, especially after the failure of the Kornilov putsch. The soldiers no longer understood why the socialist ministers spared the guilty generals, and they then lost all faith in Kerensky's loyalty to the revolution.

Stigmatizing all those leaders who had not known how to carry out the expected reforms, the soldiers impatiently clamored for the conclusion of peace. But now they also demanded the abolition of private property, distribution of land to the agrarian committees, workers' control of factories, compulsory labor and military service for all — in other words, implementation of the social revolution of which no mention had been made six months earlier. They had no doubt that accomplishment of this program was linked with the taking of power by the Soviets and its legitimation by the Constituent Assembly.

As disappointment followed disappointment the soldiers were gradually transformed into citizen-soldiers. Six months of revolution had taught them how a ruling class could wrongly identify itself with the fatherland and thus impose obligations on other social groups. They were yet to discover that in the name of socialism or revolution other leaders could just as easily seize power and use the same methods.

## I. I. Mints

# LENIN'S REVOLUTIONARY LEADERSHIP

*I.I. Mints (1896- ) is probably the foremost Soviet chronicler of Russian revolutionary history, and certainly the historian with the greatest political influence in determining the official Soviet historical view of the Revolution of 1917. A Communist since 1917, he completed his studies in the Institute of Red Professors, taught in Moscow State University, and has since 1946 been a member of the Academy of Sciences of the USSR. Lenin appears in his work as a revolutionary giant in whose hands rested the fate of the proletarian revolution. In the passage below, Mints examines Lenin's program for armed insurrection and its importance for the success of the October Revolution, arguing that other "legalist" party leaders such as Kamenev and Trotsky were incapable of real revolutionary action.*

BETWEEN September 12 and 14, Lenin wrote two letters: The first, "The Bolsheviks Must Seize Power," sent to the Central Committee and to the Petersburg and Moscow committees of the Bolshevik party; the second, "Marxism and Insurrection," sent to the Central Committee. Lenin analyzed with marvelous power and persuasiveness the internal and international situation of the country, and spelled out with great precision the conclusions and the practical proposals which followed from the analysis. "Having obtained a majority in the soviets of workers' and soldiers' deputies in both capitals,"[1] Lenin wrote in his first letter, "the Bolsheviks can and *must* take state power into their own hands." They could do so because the active majority of the revolutionary popular elements in both capitals was sufficient to win the support of the masses, to crush the opposition of the counterrevolution, and to conquer and hold power. The support of the majority of the people would be assured since the new government would immediately propose a democratic peace, give land to the peasants, and establish democratic institutions and freedom.

V.I. Lenin showed in the letter that the Bolsheviks not only could seize power but ought to do so immediately. Why? In the first place, because the counterrevolution was preparing to hand Petrograd over to the Germans, in order to suppress the city's proletariat. In the second place, because the international imperialists would overcome their conflict under the threat of the growing revolutionary movement, would conclude a separate peace and would attack with their combined forces the Russian revolution.... In the third place, power had to be seized immediately since the masses were tired of the waverings of the SRs and the Mensheviks and a decisive move by the Bolsheviks would win the support of the lower classes. Thus Lenin emphasized in his

---

1. Resolutions supporting Bolshevik policies were supported for the first time in the Petrograd and Moscow soviets in early September — Ed.

From I.I. Mints, *Istoriia velikogo Oktiabria* [The history of Great October], vol. II: *Sverzhenie Vremennogo pravitel'stva. Ustanovlenie diktatura proletariata* [The overthrow of the Provisional Government. The establishment of the dictatorship of the proletariat] (Moscow, 1968), pp. 915-917, 920-921, 923, 930-933, 945-949, 951-955. Translated by the editor.

67

letter not only the inevitability of insurrection, but its necessity as well. In this first letter on the insurrection he also raised the question of the organs of revolt, of the "apparatus" for its achievement. "Does there not exist an apparatus?" he asked, anticipating the possible objections of opponents of an insurrection. His answer was: "An apparatus exists — the soviets and the democratic organizations."

These instructions by Lenin disprove the false declaration by Trotsky, disseminated by contemporary anticommunists, that Lenin purportedly sought to achieve the insurrection without the soviets, "behind the backs" of the soviets. The slanderous character of such affirmations becomes absolutely clear if one takes into account the fact that Lenin himself in 1905 described the soviets, which had just arisen in the country, as organs of insurrection.

While calling on the party to organize the insurrection, Lenin did not indicate a date or moment for action; this question had to be decided by the Central Committee in accord with actual conditions. The immediate task was for the party to understand clearly the necessity of practical preparations for the insurrection. "The problem is," wrote Lenin, "to make clear this *task* to the party, to put on the order of the day *armed insurrection* in Moscow and Petrograd, the conquest of power, the overthrow of the government, to consider *how* to agitate for this without revealing ourselves in the press." Lenin ended his letter "The Bolsheviks Must Seize Power" with the assertion that both within and outside the country favorable circumstances were developing for a successful insurrection. "By seizing power at once both in Moscow and in Petrograd...," Lenin concluded confidently, "we will win *undoubtedly* and *unconditionally.*"

After the party had set its course toward the preparation of an armed insurrection, Lenin considered it necessary for party organizations to take up seriously one of the basic conclusions of Marxism — that insurrection is an art. The unique characteristic of Marxism in the unity of theory and practice. When setting before the proletariat the task of liquidating bourgeois society, Marx and Engels studied in detail the question of the means and form of its achievement. On the basis of the study of the experiences in revolutionary struggles of the masses, and of their own participation in the revolution, the founders of marxism developed the theory of armed insurrection.... Lenin's contribution consisted of the reestablishment of the neglected theories of the founders of Marxism on insurrection and of freeing them from distortions. Lenin went even further, however. Proceeding from the concrete experience of the new historical era, he elaborated a Marxist doctrine of insurrection and created a well-balanced theory of armed insurrection.

... During the First World War, at a time when revolution was rapidly approaching, Lenin repeatedly turned to questions of the preparation of armed insurrection — this just war of the oppressed against the enslavers. He summarized the basic conclusions of his study in his well-known article "The Military Program of the Proletarian Revolution." It indicated that revolutionary Marxists cannot be opponents of any war. They resist unjust, imperialist wars of conquest, but support just wars, including civil wars. Lenin wrote that "a civil war is also a war.... Whoever recognizes class struggle must also accept civil war, which represents in any class society the natural and in certain circumstances the inevitable continuation, development, and intensification of the class struggle." He added that there had never been a major revolution without civil war, and whoever did not recognize this lapsed into extreme opportunism and repudiated socialist revolution. Since civil war is also a form of war, it required both military knowledge and the need to be studied as a military art.

Lenin came to the October Revolution splendidly prepared theoretically, enriched by the best practical experience in the affairs of organizing and conducting an armed insurrection. The results of his theoretical findings on this question appeared in the letter mentioned above to the Central Committee, "Marxism and Insurrection." Lenin assimilated the ideas of the founders of Marxism, as well as the lessons of many insurrections and the experience of the Bolshevik party, and formulated three laws or basic conditions for a successful insurrection: "To be successful, an insurrection must rely not on a conspiracy or a party, but on a progressive class. This is the first point. An insurrection must rely on the *revolutionary upsurge of the masses*. This is the second point. An insurrection must rely on that *key moment* in the history of a growing revolution when the activism of the leading ranks of the people is strongest and when the *hesitations* among the ranks of the enemies and of the *weak, half-hearted, indecisive friends of the revolution* are greatest. This is the third point."

Comparing the situation in September and in July, 1917, Lenin showed that these conditions did not exist in the July Days, and that therefore an insurrection in July would have been a mistake. In September, the very development of objective events placed insurrection on the order of the day, since all the necessary conditions for its triumph had appeared. "All the objective prerequisites for a successful insurrection are at hand," wrote Lenin. "We have before us the exclusive benefits of a position in which *only* our victory in the insurrection will put an end to the waverings torturing the people...; when *only* our victory in the insurrection will immediately give the peasantry land; when only *our* victory in the insurrection will frustrate the plans for a separate peace against the revolution by leading to a public proposal for a more just, more complete, more immediate peace for the good of the revolution."

Only a successful insurrection of the workers of Petrograd, Moscow, and other cities could save the revolution; save Russia from partition by imperialists of both camps, preparing a separate peace for this purpose; and save Petrograd, which the counterrevolution was ready to abandon to the Germans.

... Lenin's letters have exceptional significance. First, in them he described the new political circumstances and defined the moment of ... objective preparedness for insurrection. Second, he showed in them that the Bolsheviks, unlike the opportunist movements, regarded the insurrection as an art. Third, Lenin indicated how the entire tactics of the party had to be altered in connection with the organization of the insurrection, which theoretical positions of Bolshevism required alteration in the new conditions. Fourth, he noted the essential points for the insurrection: Petrograd and Moscow with its surrounding region. Fifth, the leader of the revolution worked out the plan for the insurrection in Petrograd and defined its slogans.

... Lenin wrote articles and letters on the question of the preparations for the insurrection and sent them to the largest party organizations. In each one of these works, based on new material, he introduced supplementary arguments in support of armed insurrection, refined and expanded his practical proposals, explained the slogans of the party, and unmasked and refuted the objections of opponents of the insurrection. All in all, Lenin's works from this period of the organization of the attack on bourgeois power represent a real encyclopedia in which are laid out and clarified all the fundamental questions of an armed insurrection, from its general meaning to a concrete plan for its implementation.

Lenin attacked with particular force the opponents of an immediate insurrection who referred to the need for receiving a formal majority in the Congress of Soviets or for waiting until the Constituent Assembly.[2] On September 25 a meeting of the Petrograd Soviet was held in which Kamenev delivered a report on the current situation. The governmental crisis which had continued since Kornilov's uprising had just ended; Kerensky had reached an agreement for the entry into his government of representatives of the bourgeoisie.[3] After having discussed

---

2. The Second Congress of Soviets was scheduled to meet in October; the elections for the Constituent Assembly were to occur in November — Ed.
3. After a prolonged political crisis, Kerensky had succeeded on September 25 in reforming the Provisional Government on the basis of yet another coalition of socialists and Cadets — Ed.

the creation of the new coalition government, Kamenev declared that this was a signal for civil war. "Is there a means to head off the civil war toward which the government is leading us?" he asked. His answer: "There is! We must as soon as possible inform this government and those in sympathy with it that we refuse to grant it any support and will try to raise up against it the true source of governmental authority, the Congress of Soviets and to create there a government which the workers, soldiers, and peasants will trust to do their work and not to defend the interests of the bourgeoisie." The demand for the overthrow of the government by peaceful, "legal" means, by the formation of a government by the Congress of Soviets, was clear proof of the degree to which Kamenev was a prisoner of "parliamentary cretinism," was infected with "legalism," a faith in the legal forms of political struggle.

Trotsky spoke at this same meeting of the Petrograd Soviet. In conjunction with Kamenev's report he presented a resolution which stated: "We express our absolute certainty that news of the new government will be met on the part of all revolutionary democrats with only answer — 'resign!' And on the basis of this unanimous opinion of real democracy, the All-Russian Congress of Soviets of Workers' and Soldiers' Deputies will create a real revolutionary government." Trotsky's resolution expressed the same "parliamentary cretinism" — even the language was restrained in the spirit of a "peaceful" change in the composition of the government. The government needed to be overthrown by armed force, but Trotsky was proposing that it resign. Obviously, it was impossible to call out for an insurrection in an open meeting.... To assert, however, that it was necessary to wait for the Congress of Soviets, that this group alone had the right to legitimize governmental power, meant to divert the masses from the insurrection and to spread among them "constitutionalist illusions."

... V.I. Lenin immediately responded to these moves of the opponents of insurrection. On the same day, September 27, ... he wrote a letter to the chairman of the regional committee of the army, fleet, and workers of Finland, I.T. Smilga. "The Petrograd Soviet and the Bolsheviks have declared war on the government. The government has troops, however, and is *systematically* readying itself.... What are we doing? Are we only passing resolutions? We are wasting time by setting dates (the Congress of Soviets meets October 20 — isn't it ridiculous to delay so and to depend on this?).." Lenin went on to write that "history has made the fundamental political question now the military question. I am afraid that the Bolsheviks are forgetting this, are distracted by the 'topics of the day,' by petty current questions, and 'hope' that 'a wave will carry Kerensky away.' It is a naive hope to rely on a 'perhaps.' On the part of the party of the revolutionary proletariat this could turn out to be a crime."

What was the danger of the line proposed by the "legalists?" In the first place, it allowed the government to gather together its forces before the calling of the Congress of Soviets and thereby placed in grave danger the impending insurrection.... In the second place, by putting off the question of power until the calling of the Congress of Soviets the "legalists" gave initiative and freedom of maneuver to the leaders of the SRs and the Mensheviks, who for the time still controlled the Central Executive Committee[4] of the soviets of workers' and soldiers' delegates.... At the core of the ruinous line of the "legalists" lay an absolutely incorrect assessment of the period and of the application of methods and forms of struggle, suitable to certain conditions, to completely different circumstances. There had been a moment (during the peaceful development of the revolution) when the First Congress of Soviets could have proclaimed itself in power, and no one would have prevented this since strength was on the side of the masses and arms were in the hands of the working classes. The Provisional

4. Elected by the First Congress of Soviets in June — Ed.

Government had no armed support. The situation changed radically with the end of the peaceful period of the revolution. The Provisional Government had under its command armed forces. Were the Second Congress of Soviets to proclaim itself in power, the Provisional Government could refuse to obey and disband it by force. . . . In the new conditions, to transfer power to the soviets it was necessary not "to vote" or "to wait," but to overthrow the dictatorship of the bourgeoisie, represented by the Bonapartist-Kornilovite government of Kerensky.

. . . Let us summarize our remarks . . . on Lenin's plan for an armed insurrection. His plan foresaw not the organization of separate actions, but the transformation of isolated, spontaneous uprisings, already occurring in the country, into a general mass insurrection with the aim of overthrowing the dictatorship of the bourgeoisie. Lenin considered that the insurrection itself had to be conducted in Petrograd. . . . One of Lenin's basic conditions was not to wait for the Congress of Soviets and thereby not to inform the opponent of the moment of the insurrection or to allow him to prepare his forces for this moment.

. . . The seizure of Petrograd would come by means of an unexpected and swift blow from within and from without, leading first of all to the capture of the most important points: the telephone and the telegraph (in order to deprive the opponent of his communications with the country), and the railroad stations and bridges, which Lenin considered of prime importance since otherwise the main military strength — the worker brigades and the Red Guards — would be cut off from the center. Every district of the city had to be considered for the seizure later of government buildings, prisons, and military schools, in order to isolate those parts from which the government might call up aid from Cossacks, cavalry, and "special forces." The plan for the occupation of the city also included the capture of the major state and private printing presses, to provide the insurgents with the possibility of printing newspapers, broadsides, posters, and orders. For the sake of the rapid seizure of key points, special brigades of the most daring revolutionary soldiers, workers, and sailors were to be formed.

The entire course of the attack must have an aggressive, offensive character, . . . a systematic, energetic, and decisive offensive. It alone would bring confusion into the ranks of the opponent, would generate constant "moral superiority" among the insurgents. The insurrection had to rely not on a conspiracy or a party, but on the working class, on the lower classes. Therefore Lenin attached great importance to agitation. He recommended that at meetings and assemblies the tasks and slogans of the party be explained, that agitators be sent to wavering groups, among the Cossack regiments, in order to tear them from the influence of their officers or to neutralize them, not allowing them to bring aid to the opponent.

An insurrection is civil war and, like any war, is conducted according to the demands of military science and art. In addition, however, civil war is the highest and sharpest form of class warfare, of armed struggle of one part of society against another. Like class warfare it is subject to the laws of political struggle. The plan for insurrection was conceived and worked out by Lenin on the basis of his great experience in the leadership of the masses, his political command and awareness of military science.

. . . In the period since September 12-14 when Lenin first raised the question of the organization of the insurrection [until early October] scarcely three weeks had passed, but in a revolution every day is worth many months. Earlier, Lenin had not yet raised the question of the precise time of the insurrection, proposing that this question be resolved by the Central Committee in accord with the situation in the country. As the time passed, however, the revolution had made yet another step forward in its development. Internal and external conditions had changed. . . . Lenin considered that the moment had come when all forces had to be moved into battle. The Central Committee met on October 10, where Lenin appeared for the first time since the July Days (over three months earlier).[5] He came disguised, with a wig and no whiskers or mustache, and with a passport under the name of Konstantin Petrovich Ivanov.

The report for the Central Committee on the current situation was made by Lenin, who outlined the internal and external circumstances. In making his conclusions from the analysis of the international situation, he declared: "The international situation is such that the initiative should be in favor of us." He noted that the plans of the counterrevolution were aimed at withdrawing the soldiers from the front to the interior of the country and abandoning Petrograd to the Germans; this in particular required the shift to decisive action. Lenin emphasized that the internal situation "also pushes decisively in this direction." Comparing the current circumstances with the July Days, Lenin repeated once again that the Bolsheviks were not then in a majority, but that now a revolutionary surge had swept up all segments of the working masses. The agrarian movement had assumed massive proportions. The transferal of all land to the peasantry had become a general slogan. In the conditions of an upsurge moving with giant steps it was unthinkable to wait for the Constituent Assembly. Lenin concluded that it was time to discuss the moment of the insurrection. He stated that "the affair was completely ready (politically) for the transferal of power.... Our business now is to discuss the technical side." V.I. Lenin noted disapprovingly that "there existed a certain indifference" [within the party] to the organization of the insurrection, as a result of which "apparently considerable time has been lost" at a moment when circumstances commanded that "attention be paid to the technical side to the question." Twice in the course of his report he emphasized that the political situation was ripe for a radical change, that the issue was the precise moment of the insurrection and its technical preparation, and that it was essential to exploit any grounds for immediate action.

On finishing his report, Lenin presented his resolution on armed insurrection: "The Central Committee recognizes that the international position of the Russian revolution (mutiny in the German fleet, an extreme manifestation of the growth throughout Europe of the international socialist revolution, plus the threat of an imperialistic peace with the aim of repressing the revolution in Russia), and the military situation (the undoubted decision of the Russian bourgeoisie and Kerensky & Co. to abandon Petrograd to the Germans), and the achievement of a majority by the proletarian party in the soviets — all this, taken in connection with the peasant revolt and with the rise of popular trust in our party (the Moscow municipal elections), finally, the obvious preparations for a second Kornilovite revolt (the departure of troops from Petrograd, the arrival of Cossacks in Petrograd, and encirclement of Minsk by Cossacks, etc.) — all of this makes armed insurrection the order of the day. Recognizing, therefore, that armed insurrection is inevitable and completely mature, the Central Committee proposes that all party organizations be guided by this and adopt this point of view in discussing and deciding all practical questions (the Congress of Soviets of the Northern Region, the removal of troops from Petrograd, and action of Muscovites and Minsk inhabitants, and so on)."

A lively discussion took place on Lenin's report.... M.S. Uritsky took part in the meeting, saying that preparations for the insurrection were still insufficient. In his opinion, after the July Days the Petrograd garrison "cannot inspire great hopes"; the workers have 40,000 rifles "but this does not solve the matter for it amounts to nothing." He concluded his speech, however, with a demand for action: "We must *make up our minds* on specific action." Then Sverdlov gave information on the development of preparations for the armed insurrection throughout Russia. The issue of an immediate insurrection was so clear that Dzerzhinsky proposed "the creation in the immediate future of a Political Bureau, made

---

5. Lenin had remained in hiding since then to avoid arrest by the Provisional Government — Ed.

up of members from the Central Committee, to provide political leadership." Lenin's resolution was put to the vote. Ten members of the Central Committee voted for, two against (Zinovev and Kamenev). The resolution had become a party directive.

... At this meeting Trotsky voted for the resolution on insurrection, acknowledging that it was inevitable. That fall of 1917, however, with workers everywhere removing the old organs of government and creating revolutionary power through their struggle, with soldiers mutinying and moving with arms against governmental institutions, with landlord estates turning the sky red as they went up in flames, no one doubted the inevitability of a general insurrection (Kamenev and Zinovev also said that "an insurrection is inevitable" and that they were not opposed to action "in the future," but in actual fact they openly and violently struggled against the necessity of an insurrection). Though Trotsky voted for the resolution, he did not accept its necessity, in practice did not prepare for it, and took no part in developing the plan of insurrection. His support of the resolution remained mere words; it was not supported by active preparation for the insurrection, an indispensable step once it was recognized necessary. On the contrary, since he was entirely under the influence of constitutionalist illusions, Trotsky came out against Lenin, defending peaceful, legal, parliamentary-juridical forms of struggle such as waiting for the Congress of Soviets or for the calling of the Constituent Assembly. The real point, as shown by the course of events and as explained clearly by Lenin, was that the insurrection was not only inevitable, but it was also necessary, a pressing and real need expressing the deepest and most fundamental interests of the working masses.

In anticommunist literature the history of the preparation of the insurrection is often reduced to the analysis of statements of separate individuals and the examination of isolated events. The statements of some leaders are set against those of others, emphasizing strongly and often inventing disagreements, for the purpose of proving that the party was not united on the eve of the insurrection and that its decisions represented a sort of compromise of various points of view. Lenin is portrayed as isolated, forced to move against the entire Central Committee in order to overcome its "paralyzing inertia and skepticism." Many authors indicate that only twelve members attended the decisive meeting of the Central Committee, and try to guess how the remaining members would have voted (as though the remaining members had not been questioned or had not given their opinion on such an important question as insurrection). Thus Leonard Shapiro asserts that Lenin's letters on the insurrection found no support in the Central Committee, that nine members were absent from the decisive meeting, and "calculates" that a full meeting of all members of the Central Committee "would have revealed the opposition of a fourth of the members."[6] This attempt to distort history is revealed completely groundless in the light of actual facts. Lenin wrote already in October, 1917: "Just think about this. All the Central Committee members [that is, including those absent—I. Mints] know that at the decisive meeting over ten members of the Central Committee were in attendance, a *majority of the plenum*, that even Kamenev declared at this meeting that 'this is the decisive meeting,' and that it was well known that a *majority* of the absent members of the Central Committee *did not agree* with Zinovev and Kamenev."

Bourgeois falsifiers carefully avoid the basic fact that almost 85 percent of the members of the Central Committee supported Lenin's proposal for an immediate insurrection. One can find in history few examples of similar unanimity on the eve of such a major, decisive turning point as the shift of the party to a direct attack on the old order and to the creation of a new society. This unanimity can be explained by the entire previous history of the party, and by the unity of its theoretical and organizational views, inspired and organized by the work of Lenin.

6. Leonard Schapiro, *The Communist Party of the Soviet Union* (New York, 1960), pp. 168-169.

*Robert V. Daniels*

## THE UNPREDICTABLE REVOLUTION

Robert V. Daniels (1926-   ) is professor of Russian history at the University of Vermont. Among his works on the Russian revolutionary movement are *The Conscience of the Revolution* (1960) and *The Nature of Communism* (1962). His study of the October Revolution leads him to conclude that the Bolsheviks succeeded, not because of Lenin's master plan (which his supporters refused to implement until the last moment), but because circumstances forced them into the decisive battle against a virtually powerless enemy.

THREE o'clock in the morning, October 24. The lights were still burning in the cabinet room, the resplendent Malachite Hall on the river side of the Winter Palace. Prime Minister Kerensky, meeting with his cabinet, had finally decided that the time had come to settle with the Bolsheviks. Since no reply to General Bagratuni's ultimatum[1] had come in, the cabinet authorized the arrest of the leaders of the Military Revolutionary Committee. Now the ministers had gone home, leaving Kerensky with General Bagratuni and Colonel Polkovnikov to set in motion the forces they hoped would decapitate the Bolshevik movement.

A messenger brought a note in. It was the news that no one had expected, nor scarcely desired — the Bolsheviks had, after all, accepted the ultimatum. At this late hour, Kerensky was in no mood to suspend his preparations for a preemptive attack. Taking satisfaction in the implication that "the organizers of the uprising were compelled to announce officially that they had committed an unlawful act which they now wished to retract," Kerensky nonetheless reasoned that "this was but another case of the usual delaying tactics and a deliberate deception." General Bagratuni continued to send out telephone and telegraph messages to call reliable troops into Petrograd. Colonel Polkovnikov ordered all the commissars appointed by the MRC [Military Revolutionary Committee — Ed.] removed from their units and prosecuted for any "illegal actions" they had committed. A detachment of cadets was ordered to close down the Bolshevik newspapers *Rabochi Put* and *Soldat*, on the ground that they were inciting insurrection. To preserve political balance, the government simultaneously ordered two right-wing papers shut down.

At five thirty in the morning the cadets arrived at the printing plant where *Rabochi Put* and *Soldat* were rolling off the presses, ... less than half a mile from Smolny. They stopped the presses, broke up the plates, confiscated the papers already printed, closed the shop and left it under seal, with a few policemen on guard. ...

The report of the cadets' seizure of the printing plant, recalling the fate of *Pravda* in July, seemed to confirm all the Bolsheviks' fears and warnings about a counter-revolutionary strike, and catapulted them into a frenzy of activity. By phone and

1. Ultimatum issued by Kerensky's government ordering the Military Revolutionary Committee to rescind its order taking over command of the Petrograd garrison — Ed.

Excerpts from *Red October* by Robert Daniels are used with the permission of Charles Scribner's Sons, copyright ©1967 Robert V. Daniels, pp. 132-135, 156-158, 161-164, 214-218, 223-227.

leaflet the alarm was spread for all the pro-soviet forces in the capital, and a stream of orders began to flow to the commissars of the military units and the leaders of the Red Guard to alert their forces for any eventuality. "The counterrevolutionary plotters have taken the offensive," announced one leaflet after another, without the slightest distinction between Kerensky and the rightists. "The campaign of the counterrevolutionary plotters is directed against the All-Russian Congress of Soviets on the eve of its opening, against the Constituent Assembly, against the people.... The Military Revolutionary Committee will direct resistance against the attack of the plotters. The whole garrison and the whole proletariat of Petrograd are ready to deliver a crushing blow to the enemies of the people." Garrisons in the outskirts of Petrograd were ordered to block the movement of any hostile forces into the city, "by force if necessary." Specific orders to reopen the Bolshevik printing plant went to the nearest reliable troops, the Litovsky Regiment and an engineer battalion quartered in an imposing neoclassical barracks near the Tauride Palace. The troops responded in something less than company strength and got to the press towards midmorning. They easily thrust the police guard aside and opened the premises. By eleven o'clock the workers had *Rabochi Put* rolling off the presses again.

The vigor of the MRC response unsettled its SR contingent and the cautious Bolsheviks as well. Speaking for the Left SRs, Kamkov warned, "We did not enter the MRC for an uprising. The power must be created by the Congress of Soviets." Yielding to these misgivings, the MRC adopted a statement for the press: "Contrary to all kinds of rumors and reports, the MRC declares that it exists not at all to prepare and carry out the seizure of power, but exclusively for the defense of the interests of the Petrograd garrison and the democracy from counterrevolutionary encroachments."

While the MRC was handling the emergency, the Bolshevik Central Committee met to consider the expected attempt to suppress the party and the soviet. Nine members and two candidate members assembled for their first meeting as a party body in the Smolny Institute, hitherto strictly soviet territory. Kamenev was among them; he had felt no reason to go through with his threatened resignation. Under the pressure of the morning's events, the Central Committee abandoned its prepared agenda; its first steps were to approve the dispatch of forces to reopen the newspapers and to forbid its own members to leave Smolny (probably for fear of arrest). The main policy question was relations with the All-Russian Central Executive Committee. Trotsky wanted the Bolsheviks to go to the CEC session scheduled later in the day and denounce the CEC for "undermining the cause of revolutionary democracy." Because of the closing of the newspapers Kamenev was prepared to repudiate the negotiations they had been conducting with the CEC, though he wanted to pursue talks with the Left SRs.... There was some discussion of the location of an auxiliary party headquarters in the event that government forces captured Smolny; Trotsky's suggestion to designate the Peter-Paul fortress was adopted. With this, the total recorded substance of the Central Committee's last meeting before the revolution was completed. This was the meeting which the official historiography represents as the occasion of the final decision to launch the insurrection, but there is no evidence that the Committee had anything in mind yet except to stave off the blows of the government until the Congress of Soviets convened....

Despite all the appearances of a systematic take-over, the Military Revolutionary Committee made no recorded decision for a general attack on the government before dawn on October 25. Until Lenin appeared at Smolny each move of the MRC had come in response to a government initiative — the removal of the troops to the front, the strike at the press, the raising of the bridges, the movement of troops from the military schools and the front. The Bolsheviks could still well imagine that the Congress of Soviets and their own party headquarters were prime targets of the military, so much so that they were ready to negotiate and temporize right up to the last minute. The movements of their forces were precautionary and limited. What the Bolsheviks could not calculate was that the government's forces would give way so readily, that the cadet guards would yield everywhere without a fight, that the Cossacks would refuse to come out, that the commander of the military district was perhaps betraying the Prime Minister. In short, the Bolsheviks had naturally but grossly overestimated the strength of the government, almost as much as the government had overestimated itself.

All day Lenin had been stewing and fuming in the Fofanova apartment,[2] far removed from where the action was. He knew from Antonov that the Central Committee was planning to wait for the Congress of Soviets. He was incensed to read a newspaper report that the MRC had been negotiating with Headquarters and might agree to its terms. The day's reports contained nothing but news of the government's troop moves and the soviet's defensive proclamations. Mme. Fofanova came home from work late in the afternoon with the news that the Nikolaevsky Bridge had been lifted and an impression of the confusion at the Vyborg district Bolshevik headquarters. Lenin decided that he must go to Smolny. He sent Fofanova down to the Vyborg district party headquarters to get a message to Smolny for permission for him to leave his hideout. She returned to tell him that permission was refused. Thereupon he sat down to write out an urgent appeal to his Bolshevik followers to launch the uprising he had been demanding:

Comrades:
As I write these lines on the evening of the 24th, the situation is impossibly critical. It is clearer than clear that now, in truth, a delay in the uprising is equivalent to death.

With all my power I am striving to persuade the comrades that now everything hangs on a hair, that there are questions on the agenda that are not settled by meetings or congresses (not even by congresses of soviets) but only by the peoples, by the mass, by the struggle of the armed masses.

The bourgeois onslaught of the Kornilovists, the removal of Verkhovsky, show that we cannot wait. We must, no matter what, this evening, tonight arrest the government, after we disarm the cadets (or defeat them, if they resist), etc.

We cannot wait! We may lose everything!!

Power should be seized by the Military Revolutionary Committee or — Lenin was not even sure of the MRC — "by another institution." . . .

Once again Lenin was going around the Bolshevik leadership when they dragged their feet and trying to mobilize rank and file pressure against them — though how he expected his letter to have the desired effect in the next few hours is impossible to fathom. There is, in fact, some doubt whether anyone received the letter who was in a position to act on it — at any rate, probably not the Central Committee. But the letter is a vivid revelation of Lenin's political premises: "Seizure of power is the point of the uprising; its political aim will be clarified after the seizure." Something like Bonaparte — you plunge into the battle, and then you see what happens. In any case, the decision must not be left to arithmetical democracy: "It would be a disaster of formalism to wait for the vacillating votes of October 25. The people are justified and obliged to decide such questions not by voting but by force." Again, "the proper moment" must be seized. "The government is wavering. We must finish it off no matter what." Why, if the government was collapsing? To create the kind of power that Lenin lived for but rarely admitted. Only with such a mind could he write again, for the last time, "To delay the move is the same as death."

Lenin sent Mme. Fofanova out with his letter and a second request for permission to go to Smolny. Again he was refused. He sent her out a third time, saying that he would wait for her until 11 P.M. When she returned about 10:50, Lenin had departed, leaving a note — "I have gone where you didn't want me to go." . . .

The memoirists are unusually vague and contradictory about Lenin's arrival at

---

2. Lenin's hiding place in Petrograd on the eve of the insurrection — Ed.

Smolny and the impact it had on the course of events. Obviously it must have electrified the entire soviet headquarters. There is reason to believe that Lenin, by direct command or perhaps by his mere presence, had a decisive effect in changing the orientation of his lieutenants from the defensive to the offensive.

If the operations of the MRC during the night are carefully followed, it is apparent that a marked change in tone and direction occurred after midnight. A new spirit of bold and systematic attack appeared, exemplified in orders to military units to seize outright the public institutions that were not yet under the control of the MRC. Up to this point the moves of the MRC had all been peaceful or defensive. The committee had twice turned down Lenin's idea of returning to Smolny — because they could not protect him, or feared his presence would provoke the government, or feared that he would upset their expectation of waiting for the Congress of Soviets. But the masses of men they had set in motion to counter the government already had most of the city under their control; it was no longer easy to see the distinction between defense and offense. Lenin, apparently, provided the catalyst to turn the soviets' cautious defenders into the aggressive heroes of insurrection.

One memoirist, Lomov, comes close to the probable truth. Lomov had not yet left on his mission to Moscow, and was busy at Smolny. Before Lenin's arrival, he wrote, "Neither we nor Kerensky risk taking the path of a final engagement. We wait, fearing that our forces are still not sufficiently encouraged and organized. Kerensky is afraid to take the initiative in his own hands.

"Thus things go on until eight or nine o'clock in the evening" — Lomov was off three or four hours on the time. "Suddenly Comrade Lenin appears. He is still in his wig, completely unrecognizable. Everything decisively changes. His point of view triumphs, and from this moment we go over to a determined offensive."

"To work!" said Antonov to himself when he saw Lenin. "Our leader is w͏    ͏s! Full speed ahead!"

Until he arrived at Smolny Lenin had no information that the MRC was responding to his demand to seize power before the Congress of Soviets. In all probability they were not trying to do this up to the moment of his return; they were stumbling into power all over the city, thanks only to the total ineffectiveness of the government. But it could very well be that none of them dared confess to Lenin their defensive intentions, nor did they need to, since the state of affairs looked well enough like an offensive. Lenin was still angered by the reports he had read of the MRC's agreement with Headquarters the day before. "His first question as soon as he arrived," Trotsky recalled, "was: 'Could this be true?' 'No, it's to cover up the game,' we reassured him." From that time on every Bolshevik who was in the revolution had to represent the party's hedging tactics as some sort of ruse to fool the opposition and pave the way for a coup.

The first of the new orders apparently prompted by Lenin's return was given to a member of the MRC, Lashevich. He was instructed to get troops from the Kexholm Regiment and seize the telephone exchange, the State Bank, and the Treasury. "For the MRC," Lashevich recalled, "it became clear that the moment had come to act." . . .

Led by Lashevich, the detachment moved out along the embankment of the Moika Canal around 1:00 A.M. They met a few cadet sentries and disarmed them. Nearing the telephone building, Zakharov and his men made a dash to the open entry way and captured the armored car that had been parked there. But it was useless to them: none of the men could handle its machine guns. In the courtyard of the building they met the cadet guards rushing out of the guardroom. There was a moment of tension as the hostile forces confronted each other and shouted deadly threats back and forth. Lashevich parleyed with the guard commander and reached an agreement to avoid bloodshed: the outnumbered cadets could leave with their arms, if they promised not to fight for the government. Without a shot, the Bolsheviks had the telephone office. They promptly reconnected Smolny and cut off the phones of the Winter Palace. . . .

In the meantime, by the frosty light of the moon, other small forces were occupying the remaining key points. A detachment of Kexholm troops and sailors, with some Putilov Red Guards, occupied the Central Post Office around 1:30 A.M. The Nikolaevsky station, terminus of the Moscow railroad, and the power plants were taken over by similar detachments about the same time; usually the appearance of a soviet commissar was enough to make the employees on duty recognize the new authority. At 3:30, the *Aurora* anchored at the Nikolaevsky Bridge, already closed by Red Guards and then retaken by a platoon of government shock troops. Backed by the "moral effect" of the cruiser, sailors from the shore units easily cleared away the cadet guards and secured the bridge. By now the Provisional Government was practically isolated in the Winter Palace. At last the preemptive insurrection Lenin demanded had become a reality. . . .

The October Revolution did shake the world. In the eyes of its followers and its enemies alike, it announced the final battle between the international proletariat and the worldwide system of capitalism, the fulfillment of Marx's prophecy. The October Revolution promised a new dawn in human history, a new era of liberation and equality. Its spirit and its doctrine became a new faith for millions of people all over the world, who looked to Moscow as the new Jerusalem. Fifty years afterwards, Soviet Russia still professes to embody the ideals of the revolution, though its claim to the revolutionary heritage is disputed by the radical leaders of lands won by the Gospel of October more recently.

It is only natural that an event that has aroused such commitments and antagonisms should be viewed by both its heirs and its enemies alike as the result of deep historical forces or a long-laid master scheme. Since the days of the October uprising itself, it has been difficult for either side to take stock of the extraordinary series of accidents and missteps that accompanied the Bolshevik Revolution and allowed it to succeed. One thing that both victors and vanquished were agreed on, before the smoke had hardly cleared from the Palace Square, was the myth that the insurrection was timed and executed according to a deliberate Bolshevik plan.

The official Communist history of the revolution has held rigidly to an orthodox Marxist interpretation of the event: it was an uprising of thousands upon thousands of workers and peasants, the inevitable consequence of the international class struggle of proletariat against bourgeoisie, brought to a head first in Russia because it was "the weakest link in the chain of capitalism." At the same time it is asserted, though the contradiction is patent, that the revolution could not have succeeded without the ever-present genius leadership of Lenin. This attempt to have it both ways has been ingrained in Communist thinking ever since Lenin himself campaigned in the name of Marx for the "art of insurrection."

Anti-Communist interpretations, however they may deplore the October Revolution, are almost as heavily inclined to view it as the inescapable outcome of overwhelming circumstances or of long and diabolical planning. The impasse of the war was to blame, or Russia's inexperience in democracy, or the feverish laws of revolution. If not these factors, it was Lenin's genius and trickery in propaganda, or the party organization as his trusty and invincible instrument. Of course, all of these considerations played a part, but when they are weighed against the day by day record of the revolution, it is hard to argue that any combination of them made Bolshevik power inevitable or even likely.

The stark truth about the Bolshevik Revolution is that it succeeded against incredible odds in defiance of any rational calculation that could have been made in the fall of 1917. The shrewdest politicians of every political coloration knew that while the Bolsheviks were an undeniable force in Petrograd and Moscow, they had against them the overwhelming majority of the peasants, the army in the field, and the trained personnel without which no government could function. Everyone from the right-wing military to the Zinoviev-Kamenev Bolsheviks judged a military dictatorship to be the most likely alternative if peaceful evolution failed. They all thought — whether they hoped or feared — that a Bolshevik attempt to seize power would only hasten or assure the rightist alternative.

Lenin's revolution, as Zinoviev and Kamenev pointed out, was a wild gamble, with little chance that the Bolsheviks' ill-prepared followers could prevail against all the military force that the government seemed to have, and even less chance that they could keep power even if they managed to seize it temporarily. To Lenin, however, it was a gamble that entailed little risk, because he sensed that in no other way and at no other time would he have any chance at all of coming to power. This is why he demanded so vehemently that the Bolshevik Party seize the moment and hurl all the force it could against the Provisional Government. Certainly the Bolshevik Party had a better overall chance for survival and a future political role if it waited and compromised, as Zinoviev and Kamenev wished. But this would not yield the only kind of political power — exclusive power — that Lenin valued. He was bent on baptizing the revolution in blood, to drive off the fainthearted and compel all who subscribed to the overturn to accept and depend on his own unconditional leadership.

To this extent there is some truth in the contentions, both Soviet and non-Soviet, that Lenin's leadership was decisive. By psychological pressure on his Bolshevik lieutenants and his manipulation of the fear of counterrevolution, he set the stage for the one-party seizure of power. But the facts of the record show that in the crucial days before October 24th Lenin was not making his leadership effective. The party, unable to face up directly to his browbeating, was tacitly violating his instructions and waiting for a multi-party and semi-constitutional revolution by the Congress of Soviets. Lenin had failed to seize the moment, failed to avert the trend to a compromise coalition regime of the soviets, failed to nail down the base for his personal dictatorship — until the government struck on the morning of the 24th of October.

Kerensky's ill-conceived countermove was the decisive accident. Galvanizing all the fears that the revolutionaries had acquired in July and August about a rightist *putsch*, it brought out their utmost — though still clumsy — effort to defend themselves and hold the ground for the coming Congress of Soviets. The Bolsheviks could not calculate, when they called the Red Guards to the bridges and sent commissars to the communications centers, that the forces of the government would apathetically collapse. With undreamed-of ease, and no intention before the fact, they had the city in the palms of their hands, ready to close their grip when their leader reappeared from the underground and able to offer him the Russian capital in expiation of their late faintheartedness.

The role of Trotsky in all this is very peculiar. A year after the revolution Stalin wrote, "All the work of the practical organization of the insurrection proceeded under the immediate direction of the chairman of the Petrograd Soviet, Comrade Trotsky. It can be said with assurance that for the quick shift of the garrison to the side of the soviet and the bold insurrectionary work of the MRC the party is indebted firstly and mainly to Comrade Trotsky." This passage was naturally suppressed during Stalin's heyday, but after the de-Stalinization of 1956 Soviet historians resurrected it — as proof of another of Stalin's errors, overestimating Trotsky! In fact they are right, though the whole party shared Stalin's accolade at the time: Trotsky in October was at the height of his career as the flaming revolutionary tribune, yet he shied away from the outright insurrection that Lenin demanded. Trotsky exemplified the feelings of the main body of the Bolshevik leadership, eager for power yet afraid either to take a military initiative or to face Lenin's wrath. Trotsky talked revolution but waited for the Congress — until the moment of Lenin's return to Smolny. Then, like most of the party leadership, he persuaded himself that he had been carrying out

Lenin's instructions all along; any statement he had made without waiting for the Congress became, in retrospect, a political lie "to cover up the game." But in truth there was far more lying about the October Revolution after the event than before.

How important was the matter of waiting for the Congress of Soviets? What difference would it have made if Kerensky had not precipitated the fighting and the Congress had assembled peacefully to vote itself into power? Lenin, for one, believed it made a vast difference, and his view is underscored from the opposite direction by the conduct of the Mensheviks and Right SRs after the uprising. They were bitter and intransigent and unwilling to enter a meaningful coalition where they might have balanced the Bolsheviks. The Bolsheviks — a majority of them, at least — were emboldened by the smell of gunpowder, and ready to fight to the end to preserve the conquests of their impromptu uprising. The same was true of the Left SRs, reluctant though they had been for violence. Many moderates, on the other hand, were so enraged that they were prepared to join hands with the Ultra-Right, if need be, to oust the Bolshevik usurpers. If the Congress had met without insurrection — a large "if" — Russia would have remained for the time being on the course of peaceful political compromise; with prior insurrection a fact, Russia was headed on the path to civil war and dictatorship.

The October Revolution gave the impetus to the whole subsequent development of the Soviet Russian regime and the worldwide Communist movement. If the revolution had not occurred as it did, the basic political cleavage of Bolsheviks and anti-Bolsheviks would not have been so sharp, and it is difficult to imagine what other events might have established a similar opportunity for one-party Bolshevik rule. Given the fact of the party's forcible seizure of power, civil violence and a militarized dictatorship of revolutionary extremism followed with remorseless logic....

Was the October Revolution necessary, not in the sense of historical inevitability, but as a required step to achieve the revolutionaries' program? An affirmative answer to this question is the first principle of Leninism. For the moderate socialists, who shared the theoretical program, the answer was an equally emphatic no. The question itself involves a problematical assumption: did the revolutionary seizure of power in fact achieve the Bolshevik program at all? Actions do not always produce the results intended, and this is particularly true of political violence. What actually happened to the Bolshevik promises of 1917, "All Power to the Soviets," the magic triad "Bread, Land, and Peace," the ideal of "workers' control" and abolition of bureaucracy, self-determination for the peoples of Russia, the doctrine of the dictatorship of the proletariat and international civil war against capitalism? Every one of these points was decreed into law by the Second Congress of Soviets, and together they constituted the program by which the Bolsheviks justified their resistance to a coalition government and their establishment of a one-party dictatorship. But it was not many years before most of the program had been violated by its authors or their heirs. . . .

This chronicle of disappointment in the aftermath of revolution is not peculiar to Russia. The high hopes of revolution are always more than offset by the institutionalized violence that revolution begets, and by the subtle return of the hated but deep-seated characteristics of a nation's past. The distinctive thing about the Russian Revolution, compared with the other great revolutions of modern history, was the seizure and consolidation of power by the radical extremists, instead of a counterrevolutionary military or fascistic take-over. It was this unique success of the Left that was responsible for the special appeal of the revolutionary Russia as the idealized model both for social renovation in the West and for national regeneration in the East.

The Bolsheviks had a singular role both in Russian and world history, a role they would never have played without the sheer force of Lenin's personality — his determination to seize power no matter what and his unrelenting pressure on the party he had created to make it prepare to seize and hold power in defiance of the historical odds. Lenin could have disappeared from the scene at any one of a number of critical points: he could have been kept out of Russia by a more cautious German policy in April, 1917; he could have been caught crossing the border into Finland in August; he could have been recognized and arrested by the cadet patrol on the night of October 24. There was only one Lenin, and had any one of those contingencies gone the other way, his followers could not have found a substitute.

Nor would they have cared to. Lenin was always ahead of his party, pushing it always into bolder, more violent, more irreversible action than it cared to contemplate. There was an inertia, a mixture of democratic scruple and skin-saving timidity, that caused the party to lag behind whenever Lenin was not physically confronting his lieutenants to commit them to action. (The moderate socialist parties had the same qualities in greater measure and no Lenin to offset them.) In October the crucial test between the party's inertia and Lenin's drive for power was the question of an insurrection *before* the Congress of Soviets. Had it not occurred, dividing the socialist parties over the issue of violent change, the whole subsequent development of Russian politics could have been different. Here enters the greatest and most ironic contingency of all — Kerensky's desperate decision to attempt what looked like a counter-coup, but instead brought out the Bolsheviks' full forces in a panicky defense, and turned the city of Petrograd into an armed camp surrounding the Winter Palace. By this odd stroke of luck Lenin won what he had been unable to get from his party — a commitment of the revolution to violence that made dictatorship of one sort or another the only alternative....

The drift of Soviet Communism away from the inspiration of the revolution did not, however, prevent it from clinging to the revolutionary story as one of its principal sources of legitimacy. The revolution became and remains in official Soviet history "a revolution opening a new era in human history." The history of the revolution became an official myth, that had to prove and justify certain things — the inevitability of Communist Party rule in Russia; the genius of Lenin without whom the inevitable would never have come about; the iniquity of all Lenin's opponents, Bolshevik as well as non-Bolshevik; the retrospective treacherousness of Lenin's supporters, who later ran afoul of Stalin; the vacillation of Stalin, whose successors could not forego the temptations of rewriting history in turn.

# CONCLUSION

What do these readings tell us about the political struggle and mass movements in the Russian Revolution? Two points emerge clearly: one, the political heirs who sought in the first months to provide new leadership for their country had little enduring support among the masses; two, the collapse of the tsarist regime was followed in a very short time by a massive attack on the old social and economic order as well.

The first political heirs to the tsar to emerge in the February Revolution were the liberal Constitutional Democrats, principal power in the Provisional Government. They were committed to preparing the groundwork for a constituent assembly and democratic state, goals which would have, if achieved, given Russia what the Marxists called a "bourgeois democracy." In reality, they saw the new government as a wartime cabinet, freed of the incompetent tsar and able to pursue the war to a triumphant conclusion. They did not realize that these policies could only undermine the power of the government, for peace, not war, was uppermost in the minds of soldiers and workers. Because of this fatal weakness, Russia never actually completed its "bourgeois revolution."

Among the leaders of the Petrograd Soviet, there existed a more realistic appreciation of the weakness of their power. It rested entirely on the respect and faith which the workers and soldiers accorded the soviets as an institution of popular rule. The authority of the soviets rested on a kind of popular myth, inherited from the Revolution of 1905, that these extra-legal organs embodied the interests of the lower classes. The people were the real judges of these interests, however, not the leaders of the soviets. When one socialist emissary from the Petrograd Soviet went out during the February Revolution to organize the new militia force, replacing the old tsarist police, he discovered that the crowd of revolutionaries gathered around his headquarters were deciding in his place whom to give arms and how to punish counterrevolutionaries. He realized suddenly that "all the power in essence completely rested in the hands of the crowd," who were "convinced that this was truly the people's power." For several months, the urban masses heeded the commands of the Soviet's Menshevik and SR leadership, until moderation and collaboration with the liberals appeared to them a betrayal of the revolution. At that point, they turned to new leaders more attuned to their radical views.

The attitude of the peasantry toward the new political leadership was scarcely more favorable than it had been toward the tsarist regime. Rural Russia had no part in the February Revolution, either in the overthrow of the tsar or in the creation of the new government. This was the work of urban Russia, out of which might or might not come leaders willing to give the peasants what so many wanted — the landlords' land. Promises from the Provisional Government meant nothing; committees working on rural reform were judged only by results; emissaries from urban soviets trying to create ties with the villages were viewed as outsiders. The sight of these activists from the city prompted one peasant to remark that "some say one thing, some say another, but they all are bosses." The peasantry remained uncommitted to the new regime.

As the months passed, the problems confronting the Provisional Government only increased. Industrial production declined as strikes and shortages of goods shut down factories, but the regime had neither the means nor the will to take over factories and discipline workers on a large scale. Food supplies dwindled in the cities despite the grain monopoly declared by the Provisional Government, for the peasants preferred to protect their own interests. The army was unable to sustain a real offensive against Austria and Germany, though it did manage that summer to hold defensive positions. Mensheviks, SRs, and liberals all believed that Russia had to support its democratic allies, France, England, and the United States, at the moment when the military might of the Central Powers was growing dangerously great, but soldiers in the trenches understood only that peace was still far away and that new battles restored the authority of their officers. Faced with these acute difficulties, the socialist-liberal coalition governments had little time for consideration of revolutionary change and repeatedly deferred that spring and summer the calling of elections for the constituent assembly. Their inaction and powerlessness had the natural consequence, however, of strengthening the attraction of extreme political solutions to solve the dilemma of revolutionary leadership.

The commander-in-chief of the Russian army was the logical choice that summer of conservatives and even liberals who believed that the revolution had gone too far and that the restoration of public order was the first priority. General Kornilov thought that he could bring order to both the state and the army if he took the reins of power. Like so many other self-proclaimed political leaders that year, he claimed to be acting in the interests of the nation whose people he hardly knew. The lower classes believed in the revolution, while he talked of order. Kerensky properly judged the temper of the urban masses and of the soldiers when he called on them to back the government against Kornilov. He did not understand, though, that they cared little for him and his dreams of a democratic coalition. The defeat of the Kornilov *putsch* meant the end of hopes for a military dictatorship and left the Provisional Government little more than a phantom state.

The revolutionary turmoil that year revealed the depth of the hostility of the lower classes toward the wealthy and propertied classes. The revolution in the factories quickly turned into a movement to alter profoundly the capitalist order in industry. Workers backed the formation of factory committees, threw out undesirable engineers and foremen, and joined the militia forces. Their power to intervene in factory affairs and to organize mass political demonstrations was great. The workers' political extremism and hostility toward the bourgeoisie led many to support the Bolsheviks as the real revolutionary party. Factory committees and then soviets of workers' deputies provided key areas of Bolshevik strength by the fall. One does not have to view 1917 as a proletarian revolution to see in the worker movement elements of the new revolutionary order which emerged after October.

The soldiers also had their own ideas on revolution in the military. Their action, like that of the workers and peasants, was largely spontaneous, an outgrowth of their hostility toward the officers and of their revulsion against the seemingly endless war whose objectives they only poorly understood. At first, they accepted the authority of the Petrograd Soviet, believing its moderate leadership capable of achieving their demands. Disappointed in these hopes and increasingly antagonistic toward the "counterrevolutionary" officers and bourgeois government, many soldiers that fall identified their cause with that of the workers and the Bolshevik party. They shared the attitude of one soldier, overheard by the young American correspondent John Reed: "It seems like there are only two classes, the proletariat and the bourgeoisie ... and whoever isn't on one side is on the other."

How did the crisis of revolutionary leadership and the sweeping attack on the old order contribute to the Bolshevik victory in October? By the early fall a vacuum of power existed in Petrograd. The social revolution sweeping the factories and the army brought large numbers of individuals and revolutionary organizations to the side of the party; the rural revolution, on the other hand, only heightened the massive disorder in the country. The radicalism of the masses provided Lenin the justification for his demand for an armed insurrection by his party. His writings in September and October amounted to a concerted effort to radicalize his party's political tactics. His opponents within the party did have good reasons to resist their leader, for an independent Bolshevik seizure of power risked the party's becoming an isolated political force obliged to use repressive measures against other socialists and the peasant masses in order to remain in power. Lenin excluded the possibility of collaboration with other socialist parties in a soviet government, believing them traitors to the working masses. The origins of the Bolshevik one-party dictatorship lie in the decision for unilateral armed insurrection. In mid-October Lenin's political and personal hold over the party won him the backing of the Central committee for this policy. His personal triumph took place at a key moment of governmental weakness and popular disorder.

Few Russian political leaders, though, foresaw the ease with which the Provisional Government was actually toppled in late October. Bolsheviks hesitated to take decisive action, fearing the military forces of the government. Menshevik and SR leaders in the Petrograd Soviet continued to call for revolutionary democracy and the constituent assembly, true to their faith in democratic political processes. Kerensky continued to act like the political leader of revolutionary Russia, though few still obeyed the orders of the government. Among the workers and soldiers, large numbers preferred to abstain from any political action, refusing to support the old revolutionary leadership in the soviets and the Provisional Government, but unwilling to risk their lives for the Bolsheviks. As a result, the October Revolution was not really a revolution by the working classes, but rather a change in political leadership by force of arms.

Should one characterize the Russian Revolution as primarily the collapse of the old order in Russia or as the forging of a new order in the fires of revolution? The weight of opinion would seem to be with the former view. Largely leaderless, marked by popular disorder and conflict, the Russian Revolution brought to a violent end tsarist and capitalist Russia. The new Soviet order created by the Bolsheviks found elements of its structure and personnel in the mass organizations and militant revolutionaries appearing in those months, but it still had to be welded together into a stable regime in the months and years that followed. The October Revolution was only the first, tentative step toward Soviet Communism.

## Questions for Discussion

The following questions are intended to focus attention on some important topics for discussion.

1. What reasons did the liberals in the Provisional Government have in February and March to believe that they could lead the country in the formation of a constitutional democracy?

2. How was the attitude of the leaders of the Petrograd Soviet toward the new government affected by their belief that the overthrow of the tsarist regime was a "bourgeois revolution"? Do you think that the concept of "bourgeois revolution" is useful in understanding the February Revolution?

3. What effect did the war have on the choice of policies by the Provisional Government in the spring and summer of 1917?

4. What would the Provisional Government have had to do to win the support of the peasantry? Do you think it had good reasons to defer agrarian reform?

5. How would General Kornilov's chances of success have been affected by a decision on Kerensky's part to support his move to seize control of the government?

6. How did the working-class revolution facilitate the Bolshevik seizure of power?

7. How important was it to the Bolshevik party to have approved the principle of armed insurrection before its confrontation with Kerensky occurred in late October?

# SUGGESTIONS FOR ADDITIONAL READING

A voluminous amount of literature appeared in the past half-century on the Russian Revolution, and the works which have come out in recent years are inferior neither in quality nor quantity to those of earlier periods. This survey of books and articles on the revolution is not intended to be exhaustive, for it covers only those writings on major themes judged by the editor to be of particular interest. To uncover other works, the reader should consult bibliographic guides, of which the most helpful are the *American Bibliography of Russian and East European Studies* (Bloomington, Ind., published annually since 1957); Paul Horecky, *Russia and the Soviet Union: A Bibliographic Guide* (Chicago, 1965); and Robert Warth, "On the Historiography of the Russian Revolution," *Slavic Review,* XXVI (June, 1967), 247-264. The trend in Soviet studies on the revolution is examined in John Keep, "The Great October Revolution," *Windows on the Russian Past: Essays on Soviet Historiography since Stalin,* ed. Samuel Baron and Nancy Heer (Columbus, Ohio, 1976), pp. 139-156.

Numerous general studies of the revolution have been published, including some by participants. Among these, the most interesting are Leon Trotsky, *The History of the Russian Revolution* (New York, 1932), and Victor Chernov, *The Great Russian Revolution* (New Haven, Conn., 1936). The most useful brief survey of the events of 1917 remains the first volume of William Chamberlin, *The Russian Revolution* (New York, 1935). A good study of both the background and the revolution itself is Lionel Kochan, *Russia in Revolution, 1890-1918* (London, 1966). Marc Ferro has written a two-volume history of the revolution; the first volume has been translated into English as *The Russian Revolution* (Englewood Cliffs, N.J., 1972), while the second volume is available at present only in French under the title *La Révolution de 1917. Octobre: Naissance d'une société* (Paris, 1976). Detailed information on specific topics related to the revolution can be found in *The Modern Encyclopedia of Russian and Soviet History,* five volumes to date (Gulf Breeze, Fla., 1976-    ).

The political background to the conflict which erupted in February, 1917, has been examined from the point of view of the royal family in Robert Massie, *Nicholas and Alexandra* (New York, 1967). Two studies of the parliamentary forces and their relations with the tsar are Geoffrey Hosking, *The Russian Constitutional Experiment: Government and Duma, 1907-14* (Cambridge, 1973), and Raymond Pearson, *The Russian Moderates and the Crisis of Tsarism, 1914-17* (New York, 1977). The most detailed study of the last years of the tsarist regime is Michael Florinsky, *The End of the Russian Empire* (New Haven, Conn., 1931). Various perspectives on the political, cultural, and economic evolution of Nicholas' Russia are provided in Theofanis Stavrou, ed., *Russia Under the Last Tsar* (Minneapolis, Minn., 1969).

The February Revolution has received less attention than that of October. One tendentious study seeking to prove that the fall of the tsar was the work of a conspiracy is George Katkov, *Russia 1917: The February Revolution* (New York, 1967). Paul Miliukov's role in the revolution and in the Provisional Government can be studied in Thomas Riha, *A Russian European: Paul Miliukov in Russian Politics* (Notre Dame, Ind., 1969), and his memoirs are now available in English as *Political Memoirs, 1905-17* (Ann Arbor, 1967). A new interpretation of the process by which the mass demonstrations led to revolution is found in Tsuyoshi Hasegawa, "The Problem of Power in the February Revolution," *Canadian Slavonic Papers,* XIV (Winter, 1972), 611-632.

Two detailed histories of the soviets have appeared in English in recent years: Oskar Anweiler, *The Soviets: The Russian*

*Workers, Peasants, and Soldiers Councils, 1905-1921* (New York, 1974); and the Soviet historian A. Andreyev's *The Soviets of Workers and Soldiers Deputies on the Eve of the October Revolution, March-October, 1917* (Moscow, 1971). The Petrograd Soviet's first key effort to democratize the army is examined in John Boyd, "The Origins of Order #1," *Soviet Studies*, XIX (January, 1968), 359-372.

The activities of the Menshevik and Socialist Revolutionary parties in 1917 have not been the subject of extensive studies. The SRs have fared best, thanks to the work of Oliver Radkey, *The Agrarian Foes of Bolshevism: Promise and Default of the Russian Socialist Revolutionaries, February to October 1917* (New York, 1958). The Menshevik leader Julius Martov has been the subject of a biography by Israel Getzler, *Martov* (Cambridge, 1967). The political life of Irakli Tsaretelli is studied in W.H. Roobol, *Tseretelli — A Democrat in the Russian Revolution* (The Hague, 1976). Some documentary materials on the Mensheviks in the 1917 Revolution are contained in Leopold Haimson, ed., *The Mensheviks: From the Revolution of 1917 to the Second World War* (Chicago, 1974).

Russia's place in the wartime alliance and her diplomatic efforts in 1917 to find a way out of the war can be examined in both memoirs and secondary studies. Leading Western diplomats wrote accounts of their personal experiences, among which the most informative are Sir George Buchanan, *My Mission to Russia and Other Diplomatic Memoirs*, 2 vols. (Boston, 1923); and Maurice Paléologue, *An Ambassador's Memoirs*, 3 vols. (London, 1923-25). U.S. diplomatic relations with Russia during 1917 are examined in the first chapters of George Kennan, *Soviet-American Relations, 1917-1920*, vol. I: *Russia Leaves the War* (Princeton, N.J., 1956). There are two informative histories of Russian diplomacy that year, one by Robert Warth, *The Allies and the Russian Revolution* (Durham, N.C., 1954), the other by Rex Wade, *The Russian Search for Peace* (Stanford, 1969).

The significance of the war and the impact of the army on the development of the revolution have yet to be studied in any major historical work. The general evolution of military operations on the eastern front during the entire war is the subject of Norman Stone, *The Eastern Front, 1914-1917* (New York, 1976). The operations of the Russian army are examined in Nikolai Golovin, *The Russian Army in the World War* (New Haven, Conn., 1931). As a contrast to Ferro's article quoted in this book, one should read Allan Wildman, "The February Revolution in the Russian Army," *Soviet Studies*, XXII (July, 1970), 3-23. The June offensive is studied from the point of view of the military strategists in the High Command in Robert Feldman, "The Russian General Staff and the June 1917 Offensive," *Soviet Studies*, XIX (April, 1968), 526-542. In the first chapters of Robert Luckett, *The White Generals: An Account of the White Movement and the Russian Civil War* (New York, 1971), one can follow the growing political involvement of the army officers in late 1917. The most interesting memoirs left by a Russian officer active in the 1917 events are those of General Anton Denikin, *The Russian Turmoil* (London, 1922).

The Bolsheviks are the most exhaustively studied political group of 1917. Among the important histories of the party, one can read Adam Ulam, *The Bolsheviks* (New York, 1965); and Leonard Schapiro, *The Communist Party of the Soviet Union*, rev. ed. (New York, 1971). Alexander Rabinowitch has written two careful studies of the activities of the Bolshevik organizations in Petrograd at key moments in 1917 in *Prelude to Revolution: The Petrograd Bolsheviks and the July 1917 Uprising* (Bloomington, Ind., 1968), and *The Bolsheviks Come to Power: The Revolution of 1917 in Petrograd* (New York, 1976). The most objective biography of Lenin is David Shub, *Lenin* (Baltimore, 1966). Isaac Deutscher's admiration for Leon Trotsky leads him to overstate the young Marxist's leadership in the October Revolution and to minimize his earlier disagreements with Lenin in *The Prophet Armed: Trotsky, 1879-1921* (New York, 1954), still a fascinating account of Lenin's

# SUGGESTIONS FOR ADDITIONAL READING

closest collaborator in 1917. A recent interpretive biography of Joseph Stalin, with material on his activities in the revolution, is Robert Tucker, *Stalin as Revolutionary, 1879-1929* (New York, 1973). The interested reader will find in translation the bitter attacks on Lenin and armed insurrection, written in the fall and winter of 1917 by an erstwhile Bolshevik sympathizer and Marxist intellectual, Maxim Gorky, in his *Untimely Thoughts* (New York, 1968). Lenin's opponents in the Central Committee that fall, Zinoviev and Kamenev, are currently experiencing a sort of rehabilitation in the West, one example of which can be found in Myron Hedlin, "Zinoviev's Revolutionary Tactics in 1917," *Slavic Review*, XXXIV (March, 1975), 19-43.

A comprehensive study of the national revolutions in 1917 is provided in Richard Pipes, *The Formation of the Soviet Union* (Cambridge, Mass., 1964). The efforts of Ukrainian political leaders to found a Ukrainian nation-state are described in John Reshetar, *The Ukrainian Revolution* (Princeton, 1952). The complex struggle among Caucasian and Transcaucasian peoples is outlined in Firuz Kazemzadeh, *The Struggle for Transcaucasia, 1917-1921* (New York, 1951).

The most complete account of the social revolution in Russia in 1917 is John Keep, *The Russian Revolution: A Study in Mass Mobilization* (New York, 1976), excerpts from which the reader has already studied. In addition, one can read Lancelot Owen, *The Russian Peasant Movement, 1906-1917* (New York, 1963). An account of the impact of the revolution on certain social groups is Roger Pethybridge, *The Spread of the Russian Revolution* (London, 1972). A study of the role of the very important railroad workers' union in the revolution is W. Augustini, "Russia's Railway Men, July-November 1917," *Slavic Review*, XXIV (December, 1965), 666-679.

In addition to the memoirs already cited, there exists a vast library of personal accounts of life in Russia in 1917. A good sampling of these can be found in Dimitri von Mohrenschildt, ed., *The Russian Revolution of 1917: Contemporary Accounts* (New York, 1971). The most vivid story of the political struggles in Petrograd is Nikolai Sukhanov, *The Russian Revolution, 1917* (New York, 1955). Alexander Kerensky has written extensively and bitterly of his period of leadership in the revolution in *The Catastrophe* (New York, 1927), *The Crucifixion of Liberty* (New York, 1934), and *Russia and History's Turning Point* (New York, 1965). The views of another participant in the Provisional Government are provided by Vladimir Nabokov (father of the novelist) in *The Provisional Government* (Ithaca, N.Y., 1970). Two contrasting accounts of the October Revolution can be found in S. Melgunov, *The Bolshevik Seizure of Power* (Santa Barbara, Calif., 1972), and John Reed, *Ten Days That Shook the World* (New York, 1919). The turmoil of that year as it affected the average Russian is well captured in Konstantin Paustovsky, *The Story of a Life* (New York, 1964).

The epic scale of the revolution has naturally attracted Russian novelists. The best known of these is undoubtedly Boris Pasternak, *Doctor Zhivago* (New York, 1958). A glimpse of the violence of the revolution among the Don Cossacks is Mikhail Sholokov, *The Silent Don* (New York, 1934). A fictional view of the revolution in the cities is provided by Alexis Tolstoi, *The Road to Calvary* (New York, 1946), also known as *Ordeal* (Moscow, 1953). Alexander Solzhenitsyn has just begun his own multi-volume vision of the collapse of the old order and the revolution, the first volume of which is *August, 1914* (New York, 1972).

Several extensive collections of documents from the revolution are available in English translation. Two of particular use are Robert Browder and Alexander Kerensky, eds., *The Russian Provisional Government 1917*, three vols. (Stanford, 1961); and Martin McCauley, *The Russian Revolution and the Soviet State: Documents, 1917-21* (New York, 1975). A sampling of Lenin's writings is provided in Robert Tucker, *A Lenin Anthology* (New York, 1975).

The Russian Revolution has appeared very differently to various people at various times and places. Contemporary press accounts in the United States are gathered together in *Revolution in Russia as Reported by the N.Y. Tribune and the New York Herald* (New York, 1967). American liberals had their own ideas of the significance of events in Russia in 1917, as is apparent in Christopher Lasch, *The American Liberals and the Russian Revolution* (New York, 1962). In the Soviet Union, the history of the revolution is inextricably bound to the Marxist-Leninist interpretation of Russia's past, present, and future, as well as to the political needs of the party leaders at a particular time, as studied by Nancy Heer, *Politics and History in the Soviet Union* (Cambridge, Mass., 1971). The particular synthesis which I.I. Mints has made of Marxism-Leninism and the events of 1917 is the subject of an article by Alan Kimball, "I.I. Mints and the Representation of Reality in History," *Slavic Review*, XXXV (December, 1976), 715-723. One Russian philosopher, Nicholas Berdiaev, found the roots of Bolshevism in his country's past in *The Origins of Communism* (New York, 1948). Two books place the Russian Revolution in the European perspective: Crane Brinton compares it with the French, British, and American revolutions in *The Anatomy of Revolution* (New York, 1965); and Adam Ulam looks for the causes of the revolution in the dynamics of industrialization in *The Unfinished Revolution* (New York, 1960). Theodore Von Laue views the revolution as one step in the Russian process of adapting to the pressures of Westernization, in *Why Lenin, Why Stalin: A Reappraisal of the Russian Revolution, 1900-1930* (New York, 1971).